# Evolution, Marxism and Christianity
## Studies in the Teilhardian Synthesis

This is Volume Two in *The Teilhard Study Library*, which examines different aspects of the thought of Teilhard de Chardin and considers its implications for the future of man.

These are the texts of papers given at the first annual conference of The Teilhard de Chardin Association of Great Britain and Ireland which was held, under the title of this book, in London in October 1966. Reflecting a full dialogue, among people of different fundamental beliefs and intellectual disciplines, which Teilhard's thought makes possible, the six papers appear in the order in which they were delivered; those by Dr. Claude Cuénot are omitted as they form part of Volume One in the *Library*. The last chapter is a discussion which was recorded after the conference and broadcast on the Third Programme of the B.B.C. in February 1967.

A broad range of ideas is presented here, and they are accompanied by a real hope for the future of man, seen existentially as a single species engaged in a very remarkable evolutionary process.

THE TEILHARD STUDY LIBRARY

*Pierre Teilhard de Chardin Association of Great Britain and Ireland.*

# EVOLUTION, MARXISM & CHRISTIANITY

## Studies in the Teilhardian Synthesis

*Contributors*

CLAUDE CUÉNOT
F. G. ELLIOTT
ROGER GARAUDY
A. O. DYSON
P. G. FOTHERGILL
VERNON SPROXTON
BERNARD TOWERS

GARNSTONE PRESS

First published by
THE GARNSTONE PRESS LIMITED
59 Brompton Road, London S.W.3
in October 1967

*194.9*
*T264zpi*

*B2430*
*T374*
*P5*

SBN:900391 06 5

Printed by The Anchor Press Ltd., Tiptree, Essex

# Contents

# Foreword

Teilhard de Chardin never claimed to have constructed a closed and definitive system of thought which would be protected and propagated after his death by "disciples". His well-known remark, "If I have had a mission to fulfil, it will only be possible to judge whether I have accomplished it by the extent to which others go beyond me", correctly summarizes the aim and the content of his writings.

To ignore the conditional character of Teilhard's undertaking can only lead to a dogmatism and rigidity of thought which he would have been the first to disown. In an early essay on 'Creative Union' he wrote, "It is very much better to present *tentatively* a mixture of truth and error than to mutilate reality in trying to separate before the proper time the wheat from the chaff. I have followed without hesitation this Gospel rule which is the rule of every intellectual endeavour and of all scientific progress." Again, in THE VISION OF THE PAST, Teilhard insisted that, "the views that I present are still, as I said, only at their birth. Do not therefore take them as universally accepted or definitive. What I am putting before you are suggestions rather than affirmations. My principal objective is not to convert you to ideas which are still fluid, but to open horizons for you, to make you think."

Thus Teilhard attempted to sketch the provisional outline of a synthesis which would integrate the Christian Gospel with the evolutionary self-consciousness of modern man—an outline which he hoped others, from many different starting points, would correct, develop and apply.

Consequently, to be faithful to the particular character of Teilhard's achievement requires not simply detailed expositions and clarification of his thought. There are the further essential tasks, critically to determine the areas in which his thought is open to creative development, and to work out in detail the feasibility of its application to the problems which confront and inhibit the growth of human society.

It is our conviction that the interest, ferment and controversy which have surrounded Teilhard's writings since his death in 1955,

vii

mark him out not as an ephemeral and modish thinker, but rather as one whose insights and methods can, if explored with discrimination, make a more permanent contribution towards the enrichment, unification and constructive evolution of thought and action in society across existing boundaries of race, politics, religion, science, etc.

Guided by these considerations, the Editors hope that the volumes of *The Teilhard Study Library*[1] will bring such free-ranging and mature reflection upon the implications of Teilhard's *oeuvre* to the notice of a wide public.

*General Editors*
                                                    BERNARD TOWERS
                                                    ANTHONY DYSON

---

[1] Details concerning the Association, which is promoting this series of books in association with the publishers, appear on page 111.

# Introduction

This volume contains the texts of papers given at the first annual conference of The Pierre Teilhard de Chardin Association of Great Britain and Ireland held in London in October 1966. They are printed in the order in which they were given at the conference, but do not include those of Dr. Cuénot, which were placed between those of Dr. Fothergill and Dr. Towers, as they are published in fuller versions in Volume One in this series. The last chapter consists of a radio discussion, recorded after the conference by the B.B.C., and subsequently broadcast in the Third Programme.

The theme of the conference is accurately conveyed by the title of this book. It attracted an audience of over five hundred people: christians of many denominations, secular humanists and marxists. Many of those present asked for the publication of the proceedings. This was not only so that they could have a permanent record of what they regarded as a stimulating experience, but also so that the views expressed could reach a larger audience. It is relatively rare to experience real dialogue, real communication, between people of very different fundamental beliefs and from different intellectual disciplines. The genius of Teilhard appears to make such dialogue possible. With that goes a real hope for the future of man, seen existentially as a single species engaged in a very remarkable evolutionary process.

The contributors, in alphabetical order, are as follows:

CLAUDE CUÉNOT, author of many books and articles on the life and thought of Teilhard; Secretary of the Committee for the publication of Teilhard's works.

ANTHONY O. DYSON, theologian and ordained minister of the Church of England; chaplain of Ripon Hall, Oxford, where he teaches Christian Doctrine and Ethics.

FRANCIS G. ELLIOTT, of the Society of Jesus, lecturer in biochemistry at the Lovanium University of Leopoldville; he holds a degree in theology as well as a doctorate in biochemistry of the University of Louvain.

PHILIP G. FOTHERGILL, senior lecturer in botany at the University of Newcastle; author of a number of books on evolutionary theory.

ROGER GARAUDY, director of the Centre for Marxist Study and Research in Paris, member of the Political Bureau and of the Central Committee of the French Communist Party; professor of philosophy at the University of Poitiers.

VERNON SPROXTON, television producer, author, critic and ordained minister; he recently produced a television film on the life and ideas of Teilhard.

BERNARD TOWERS, lecturer in anatomy at the University of Cambridge; fellow, tutor, and director of medical studies, Jesus College, Cambridge.

After this brief indication of the backgrounds from which they spoke, the individual contributors will themselves suggest, in their papers, what it is about the thought of Teilhard that makes it possible for them to appreciate more keenly the integrity of another's approach to problems of mutual interest. With that appreciation went an increased understanding—more, even, perhaps, than they themselves had expected.

*Jesus College, Cambridge*                                              BERNARD TOWERS
*February* 1967

# CHAPTER ONE

## *The Origin of Life and the World Vision of Teilhard de Chardin: The Creative Aspect of Evolution*

by Francis G. Elliott, S.J.
Translated by Noël Lindsay

When Teilhard de Chardin sought to understand man's place in nature, he made use of the concept of evolution, which he borrowed from the vocabulary of science, but which he gave a dynamic and philosophical significance going far beyond the positive and particular meaning attached to it by palaeontologists and biologists. For them, evolutionism served to explain the origin, or, more exactly, the differentiation, of living species, including man. For Teilhard de Chardin "evolution" became the key concept for an understanding of man and his place in the Universe. Such a bold shift of meaning could be justified not only because, in the eyes of the palaeontologist, man merges "anatomically" in the mass of the Mammals, but also because the evidence had just been discovered—and at Chou kou tien Teilhard had made his own contribution—that man issued from the living kingdom by evolution, and is, indeed, its latest product. Quite naturally, he was thus inclined to accept the fact that, reciprocally, the same law implied that life itself proceeded by evolution from matter. But on this point, the science of the day could provide only vague indications, and, moreover, the still recent polemics on spontaneous generation seemed to contradict this interpretation.

At the present time, from the point of view of Teilhard de Chardin's vision of the world, the problem of the origin of life rises in two ways: is it legitimate to apply the concept of evolution to the problem of the origin of life, as has been done to explain the origin of man, and, secondly, is the teaching of science on the genesis of life from matter calculated to illuminate and enrich our thinking on evolution itself and its creative power? To give a valid answer to the first question we must, in the logical sequence of Teilhard's thought, start with the second, "what has science to say about life and its origins?". Only then can we ask whether life comes from the evolution of matter.

## LINES OF APPROACH

There are several possible lines of approach to the problem of the origin of life as it arises for science. We should like to follow here a line of thought similar to that followed by Charles Darwin in THE ORIGIN OF SPECIES in tackling the problem of the origin of animal species by evolution, and to distinguish four types of argument, based respectively on palaeontology, morphology, embryology and genetics.

Palaeontology starts by dividing history into longitudinal sections and seeking the links between species that have appeared successively in time; in considering the origin of life this becomes palaeo-biochemistry. Alternatively, it takes a cross-section at a given period and compares the morphological similarities between species; this is comparative anatomy or morphology, which has its equivalent at a microscopic level in comparative biochemistry. There is a third approach, which is particularly appropriate to the study of evolution and which to some extent combines the first two; this is the comparison of the specific dynamics of the development of organisms now living, and is called comparative embryology. Finally, the fourth line of approach is experimental evolutionism; in the case of living organisms this takes the form of genetics, and in the case of "prelife", of de la synthèse biochimique.

We shall start by considering what these different lines of approach have to teach us about the origin of life, and then go on to see, by reflection, what light they can throw on evolution and its creative aspects.

## THE DATA OF BIOCHEMISTRY

The phylogenetic study of the origin of life is made practically impossible by the disappearance of sufficiently ancient palaeontological remains and by our ignorance of the climatic and atmospheric conditions of the epoch. According to present estimates, the earth has been in existence for rather more than four and a half billion[1] years, and the

[1] American usage=thousand million. Eds.

appearance of life on earth is placed about two and a half to three billion years ago, which is also the age of the oldest rocks of the earth's crust. The earth was warmer, and the atmosphere did not yet contain oxygen, but probably methane and ammonia. The vestiges of life dating from this epoch are too uncertain to throw any light on its origin. No precise information is yet available about extra-terrestrial life. The hope of finding some traces of it in certain meteorites is still unconfirmed. It may be that the exploration of the moon and of the other planets will throw some light on life and its primitive stages.

Compared with the meagre information to be obtained from palaeontology, that obtained from comparative biochemistry is much more abundant. One fact can be singled out as especially important for our purposes, namely the extraordinary similarity in the biochemical composition of living creatures. All organisms have virtually the same *elementary composition*. They are made up of some twenty chemical elements, in almost constant proportions and practically always playing the same role: carbon, hydrogen, oxygen, nitrogen and sulphur form the basic molecules; sodium, potassium and calcium provide the positive ions, with their replica in the negative ions, chlorate, carbonate, phosphate and sulphate. Finally, half a dozen other elements are necessary, but only in minute traces, such as iron in haemoglobin and magnesium in chlorophyll. In passing, one is bound to admire the extraordinary economy of means utilized to bring about the unbelievable diversity and richness of the living world and of man. When we compare the molecular composition of cells, we find the same similarity. They all contain carbohydrates, fats and proteins, and everywhere these substances exercise the same kind of function. All organisms are aqueous systems, that is to say, solutions based on *water* and salts. The energy necessary for their activity is fixed in the form of *carbohydrates*, stored and transmitted in this form, before being used by the organism itself or by other organisms. The *fats* have a similar role to the carbohydrates, but they allow a longer-term and more economical storage of energy. It is nevertheless becoming clearer and clearer that the fats have their own very special function in the formation of membranes and of certain cellular structures indispensable to the speed and selectivity of metabolic exchanges, between one part of the cell and another, and between the cell and the external environment. The *proteins* can also supply energy and help to form the structures of the organism, but they also ensure, in the form of enzymes, the rapid and selective execution of the innumerable chemical transformations which maintain the life of the organism.

While sharing the energy function of the carbohydrates and the structural role of the fats, the proteins are first and foremost the sole organizers of the living being. We "act" thanks to the carbohydrates, the main source of energy, we "think" with the help of the fats, which make up the structure of our nervous cells, but we "exist" by virtue of the proteins which make up our substance, and we "grow old" because our proteins have aged or, in biochemical language, have become "denatured". Thus the whole problem of "prelife" is centred on the question of the origin of proteins.

Before coming to this point, however, we must consider the metabolic similarity. The biochemical mechanisms and the metabolic linkages are practically the same throughout the living world. The basic activities of our cells are to be found in all living organisms, and the enzymes are so similar that they are, in practice, interchangeable. The greater part of the biochemistry of the cells of our organism was first studied in cells of yeast and bacteria. Those differences between organisms which at first sight appear the most stubborn, come down in the last analysis to different relationships between similar metabolic pathways or to secondary variations grafted on to basically identical systems.

Comparative biochemistry thus impels us to the conclusion of the fundamental similarity between all living organisms, both in their chemical composition and in their biochemical activities. This conclusion does not yet afford proof of evolution, but it raises a strong presumption in favour of a world of living beings all issuing by evolution from one common origin.


## THE CHARACTERISTICS OF PROTEINS

In order to reach a better understanding of the origins of living matter, we must go back for a moment to proteins and look a little more closely at what might be called their phenomenological characteristics. Proteins are substances in which the apparently quite commonplace combination of a small number of elements produces chemical substances of the highest complexity and diversity which are among the most singular in existence.

The *singularity* of proteins is that they cannot be ranged with other substances. They are too large to be classed with ordinary molecules, too characteristic and too soluble to be called colloids, much too complex and, above all, too unstable to be regarded as ordinary chemical substances; their existence has a limited duration passing through a fetal state, an adult age and an old age, leading to their death, known as "denaturation", and ultimately to their decomposition. Finally, they are extraordinarily active, effective and specific in their catalytic activity. The best way of understanding how *complex* they are, and capable of the most complicated operations, is to reflect upon what we are and what we try to do. We need water, salts and carbohydrates, fats and some ordinary organic substances, but we "are" because of our proteins; what we do, we do thanks to them. To say this is in no way to exaggerate. However one looks at the matter, this conclusion is inescapable.

To appreciate the *diversity* of the proteins it is enough to think of the diversity of living species and, more particularly, of the diversity of our heredities. Even the diversification which may have been imprinted on our biochemical equilibrium by environment and education is largely reflected in the proteins of our organism.

What are they like, these substances which are so singular, so complex and so diverse? What do we know about their constitution?

As we have said, they are composed of very few chemical elements, five in all, among the hundred chemical elements known in the universe, carbon, hydrogen, oxygen, nitrogen and sulphur, elements which are found in the terrestrial atmosphere and in water. They are not found pure in proteins, but combined, to the number of fifteen to twenty, in the form of molecules of amino acids. These amino acids are fairly simple in composition; they have an acidic carboxylic group, a basic amino group, and each of them has a different radical. But, in all, there are no more than twenty different radicals. Here again, we find the astonishing economy of means which governs the building up of living matter. The number of possible arrangements of five elements in groups of up to twenty reaches, as can be imagined, astronomical figures. And yet, the number of amino acids which constitute the proteins is not more than twenty. Years of meticulous and often repeated research have only served to confirm this—the rare exceptions encountered merely suggest sports. Furthermore, the great majority of proteins of the most diverse organisms contain all the twenty amino acids, and in very similar proportions, which once again confirms the fundamental unity of all living matter. In the protein the amino acids are not assembled at random but linked together in chains of 100 to 200 units. The link between the acid group of one amino acid and the basic group of the next is called a peptide bond. The polypeptide chain thus formed is so strong that very energetic means are needed to break it in the laboratory. The organism does not experience the same difficulty, since it produces, for example in the digestive system, enzymes capable of breaking it with the greatest of ease.

But it is not every polypeptide formed from our eighteen vital amino acids that constitutes a protein—far from it. In order to form a protein the chain must not only be fairly long—at least 100 to 200 units —but it must also be *structured*.

Here we begin to understand how nature, with so few elements combined in such a simple way, can attain such complexity and such great diversity. To begin with, amino acids may always exist in two forms, similar in every point, except that they cannot be superimposed on each other, rather like left hand and right hand gloves. The biological amino acids are all of the *left hand* type, the others are unusable or toxic. This form of structure, discovered by Pasteur, is called *optical isomerism*.

Next, in the polypeptide chain, the hundred or so amino acids cannot be arranged arbitrarily; they must follow each other in a well determined order which is called the *primary structure* of the protein. The importance of this sequence has been clearly brought out in recent years by the discovery of the biochemical mechanism which causes a hereditary disease of the blood, known as "sickle-cell anaemia". In certain regions of Africa, the number of children affected by this disease —which leaves no hope of survival—may be as high as 1%. Biochemical researches inspired by Linus Pauling have shown that this particular anaemia is due to the replacement of a single amino acid by another in the sixth position of one of the two pairs of haemoglobin chains, the whole chain including some 150 amino acids. Pauling did not fail to note that, for the first time, it had been possible to locate with precision, if not the mechanism, at least the biochemical cause of a disease, and he called it "molecular disease".

In addition to the primary structure, that is to say, the composition and sequence of the amino acids, the chain must have a particular spatial configuration if there is to be a protein and not a simple polypeptide. In the first place, the chain is not simply linear or entangled but, at least in certain parts, coiled in spirals like a spring. This helical configuration determines what is called the *secondary structure*. The most decisive discoveries on this question are once again due to Pauling.

But even this is not enough. The helical structures are themselves bent back in a three-dimensional configuration known as the *tertiary structure*, the study of which has proved very complicated and has taken years of research and calculation. In recent years, however, the tertiary structure of a protein has been solved; that of the myoglobin of muscle and its relative, haemoglobin. We owe this to Kendrew and Perutz, who were awarded the Nobel Prize for this discovery. The helical chain is folded back eight times. The haemoglobin of the blood differs from myoglobin only in containing four chains of a type approaching that of myoglobin. The configuration resulting from the aggregation of several chains is called the *quaternary structure*. The model of this ball of spiral chains folded back on themselves has a somewhat disappointing appearance. Perutz has said that at first sight he was a little disappointed at obtaining, after years of work and calculations, an image of the molecule of haemoglobin in such a trivial form. "Could the search for ultimate reality," he wrote, "really have revealed so hideous and visceral-looking an object?"[1] Nevertheless, the tertiary structure is fundamental, since it is found throughout the family of haemoglobins, even in the myoglobin of the whale, which has, however, only some forty amino acids in common with human haemoglobin in equivalent positions. The reason why the tertiary structure is so vital seems to be connected with the creation of a particular environment within the molecule, distinct from the external environment, which allows the special play of reactions and exchanges proper to the behaviour of proteins.

Before coming to a conclusion on this point, it is preferable to return to the problem of the evolution of matter and to proceed to the next type of biochemical argument.

## THE ONTOGENESIS OF PROTEINS

The two foregoing types of argument were primarily descriptive, palaeontology taking a longitudinal section of time and comparative

[1] SCIENTIFIC AMERICAN, November 1964, p. 70.

B

biochemistry a cross-section. The arguments which follow adopt a more frankly dynamic point of view. The first is derived from embryology and the next from genetics. Comparative embryology has thrown a great deal of light on the process of evolution, and Haeckel derived from it his famous and highly controverted biogenetic law that the individual, in his own development (ontogenesis) recapitulates the history of his own species and all those which preceded it (phylogenesis). So far, the study of biochemical ontogenesis has not revealed the traces of former processes—the manuscript is too ancient and too overwritten—but it does reveal certain very interesting *present* facts concerning the origins of life and the *ontogenesis of proteins*. How does the cell set about receiving, so rapidly and so effectively, and without risk of error, the synthesis of such complex and delicate substances as the proteins? The problem is a very real one; the proteins of our organism are fairly unstable, and our cells are constantly renewing them, not from ready-made polypeptide chains, but from free amino acids, most of which can be synthesized by the human organism but seven of which must be supplied by food.

How do our cells succeed in rapidly and effectively assembling the desired amino acids in the requisite order to ensure that the sequence is correct? This problem intrigued biochemists for a long time, but it is only in recent years that they have succeeded in elucidating the highly ingenious and efficient mechanism. If we disregard the intermediate and subsidiary stages, and concentrate on the principle of the process, we can compare it to type-setting. The amino acid chain of a protein can be compared to a sentence, the letters of which are the eighteen proteinic amino acids. Certain amino acids even seem to play the role of spaces or punctuation marks in this sentence, separating the groups of amino acids and articulating the chain at certain points.

In the nucleus of the cell, which might be compared to the type-setting shop, there is a complete set of primary matrices, corresponding to each of the proteins which the cell may be called upon to synthesize; these are the desoxyribonucleic acids which are found on the chromosomes of the nucleus of the cell. A copying process permits the reproduction of a secondary matrix, the negative image of the primary matrix. This derived matrix, ribonucleic acid, passes from the nucleus into the cytoplasm of the cell, and settles at the spot where the proteinic synthesis is to take place. The proteinic sentence, however, should not be compared to a printed text, but rather to a string of letters. To form this chain, a system of keys, adapted on the one hand to the slots of the secondary matrix, and, on the other, to each amino acid, proceeds to select these amino acids from the cellular environment and, travelling the slots of the matrix, automatically arranges the amino acids alongside each other in the desired order. This is followed by a reaction of combination between the acidic and basic groups of the amino acids which spreads along the whole series and locks them together like a sort of zip fastener. The chain thus formed easily detaches itself from the series of bonding keys and from its matrix. The system of primary and secondary matrices and of bonding keys is not proteinic, but of the nucleic acid type. It is made up, not of amino acids, but of nucleotides, which are in turn composed of a nitrogen base, a sugar molecule and phosphate. We have known of the nucleic acids for a long time, and their presence on the chromosomes suggested that they played a part in the reproduction of living matter. But we came up against the paradox that they were composed, not of twenty elements, but only of four different nucleotides. How could four elements serve to select a group of twenty? Taken singly they give only four arrangements; taken in pairs they still only yield sixteen. The conclusion had to be that each unit of the matrix is formed of at least three nucleotides. This gives 64 possible combinations, which is too many for the twenty or so amino acids, but which is, at any rate, sufficient. In recent years a great many biochemists all over the world have been trying to break what they call the nucleic acid "code" to discover the triplet of nucleotides corresponding to each amino acid. This very arduous task of decoding has now made enough progress to allow tables of correspondence to be drawn up between the triplets of nucleic acids and the amino acids. It has also been possible partly to confirm the accuracy of the deductions by the nucleic synthesis of simple polypeptides. One hesitates which to admire the more, the ingenuity of these natural mechanisms, or the sagacity of the biochemists who succeeded in unravelling them.

The admiration felt for such an ingenious mechanism of synthesis is, however, somewhat tempered by our disappointment at finding that the problem of the origin of life has merely become more remote and more complicated. The proteins, as we have seen, are capable of all vital activities, such as assimilation, movement, etc., but the activity which is generally regarded as most characteristic of the living being, namely reproduction, is the attribute not of the proteins, but of the nucleic acids. The explanation of the origin of life by the evolution of matter thereby becomes more arduous. The proteins are necessary to the synthesis of certain constituents of the nucleic acids, but the latter play a part in the reproduction of the proteins. Which of these two fundamental substances must be given phylogenetic priority? Is the origin of life to be found in the line of the proteins, with the nucleic acids as secondary derivatives, or vice versa?

## THE PRIORITY OF THE PROTEINS: EXPERIMENTAL EVOLUTIONISM

It is hard to believe that this is a genuine dilemma, since proteins and nucleic acids are not strictly equivalent; the product is always primary compared with the mould from which it has been produced in mass. It is fairly plausible that the system of the reproduction of proteins by means of nucleic acids reflects a posterior invention in the history of life, an invention so efficient that it has completely obliterated all trace of an older but less efficient mechanism of synthesis in which the nucleic acids did not yet play any part. Since the origin of life goes back at least three billion years, it might well be accepted that the original purely proteinic process of synthesis has been entirely supplanted in our cells by the present system, with the intervention of the nucleic acids derived from the contributions of a later phase of evolution. Its traces would have disappeared in ontogenesis just as the palaeontological testimony has disappeared in the rocks.

Our object here, however, is to demonstrate that the origin of life from matter gives a better understanding of the evolution of the universe in general, and not to explain the evolution of matter by evolution in general. In order not to be trapped into begging the question we must go back to the observation of phenomena. *Experimental biochemistry* seems to offer a sound way of breaking the deadlock. This brings us to the fourth approach to the problem of the origin of species and of life, namely experimental evolutionism, genetics in one case, and the experimental biochemical synthesis of life in the present case. It is not to be expected in our days that matter should still spontaneously produce life on earth; the geological and meteorological conditions for the non-enzymatic synthesis of proteins no longer seem favourable, especially because of the abundance of atmospheric oxygen. And even if it were to happen, it is highly improbable that it would be perceived since the slightest trace of protein formed would be immediately devoured by the micro-organisms of mould. But in the laboratory, where it is possible to work in aseptic conditions and achieve the desired atmospheric environment, the synthesis *in vitro* of living matter should be possible. The most recent discoveries indicate that this is indeed feasible and that we are nearing our goal.

Among the various attempts, we shall merely single out here one line of research which, while it has not yet reached the final solution, at least sheds most light on our argument, and this precisely because of its tentative and only partially successful character. The results of these researches are regularly published and were summed up quite recently by Sydney Fox.[1] The first stage was to produce basic biological molecules, and especially amino acids, by abiotic synthesis. This was achieved quite recently by treating certain mixtures of gas in a vacuum with radiations or electric discharges. But the results were disappointing since only two or three amino acids were obtained, drowned in a variety of foreign products. Nevertheless, abiotic synthesis was proved in practice. Harada, a colleague of Fox, adopted a simpler process, starting from ammonia, water and methane gas, three volcanic derivatives which were probably fairly abundant in the primitive atmosphere. He submitted them to temperatures of the order of 1000°C, similar to those prevailing in active volcanoes, and used a bed of volcanic dust as catalyst. The results were astounding: in the reaction products he identified fourteen of the eighteen proteinic amino acids. Among those missing were the two sulphuric amino acids, and for good reason: he had been careful not to include sulphur in the reaction mixture. The absence of the sulphuric amino acids afforded proof that the amino acids formed did not come from bacterial fermentation. The two other amino acids have not yet been identified, but they may have been present. Conversely, no amino acid unknown in the proteins was ever found among the reaction products. Thus, by a very simple method, close to natural conditions, the almost complete set of proteinic amino acids has been synthesized, and no others. The biochemist who knows the hazards and complexity of synthesis reactions catches his breath in the face of such results.

The next stage was to synthesize a polypeptide. Most previous attempts had failed; amino acid derivatives had been used, or polymerization had been tried starting from a single amino acid. Fox and

[1] NATURE (London) **205**, 23rd January 1965, pp. 328–340.

Harada thought that, since the amino acid composition of all organisms is fairly similar, and their method of total synthesis had produced a complete mixture, it was better to try copolymerization on a mixture of the eighteen amino acids at once. They did this by moderate heating of the mixture for six hours at 170°C, or at 65°C in the presence of phosphate. The result was an unhoped-for success: they obtained polymers of a fairly high molecular weight—3,000 to 10,000—in which the amino acids were found combined in the same proportions as in the mixture. Not desiring to pronounce on the proteinic nature of the products, they called them "proteinoids". Their most characteristic properties are:

(1) Their composition in amino acids is comparable to that of ordinary proteins, and the beginnings of a sequence can be discerned;

(2) They can be attacked by proteolytic enzymes, one of whose properties is the ability to decompose proteins;

(3) In a culture medium they allow the development of micro-organisms; they are therefore edible;

(4) The proteinoids are capable of metabolic activity, since they catalyze biochemical reactions, on the model of enzymatic proteins. Three well identified cases of such catalysis have already been described.

It will be noted that the properties listed above fall within the domain proper to proteins and are essential to life.

The third step was to lead to the segregation of cellular type units and the formation of membranes. Here again, the proteinoids proved themselves front-rank imitators, so successful as to be somewhat disturbing. Quite ordinary physico-chemical treatments disintegrate them into spherules of about 2 microns in diameter, that is to say, the same dimensions as spherical bacteria. Under the electron-microscope the image of sections of these proteinoid spherules shows an internal structure and the formation of a membrane. The membrane is even formed of a double layer similar to that discovered not so long ago in the intracellular corpuscles, whose very constant thickness and structure throughout the living world has strongly aroused the attention of cytologists. Finally, to crown this masterpiece of imitation, it has been possible to observe and photograph under the microscope figures of spherule division by bi-partition, similar to certain forms of cellular division.

The sheaf of resemblances and analogies listed above, however, does not yet allow us to claim the proteinoids as genuine proteins. They still lack a great deal; it has not been shown that the structure is strictly uniform; nothing is known about the tertiary structure; they are not composed of optically active amino acids; enzymatic activity, while real enough, is not as powerful as that of ordinary enzymes. But the analogies mentioned are enough to show that, if the proteinoids are not the authentic prototypes of prelife, they can nevertheless be regarded as a new approach, a rebirth, which could, under appropriate conditions of space and time, constitute a fresh start for matter emerging into life.

There remains the question of reproduction. Research on the proteinoids has not yet revealed anything on this subject, apart from the division images mentioned above. It must not be forgotten that this research is very recent and is just beginning. Although it has not yet been possible to show a power of reproduction in the proteins themselves, it is likely that they initially possessed it, and that the reproduction of proteins through the medium of the nucleic acids is only a later invention conferring a particular function of life on a special substance better qualified for the task, just as, in the higher animals the reproductive function proper to each cell has been lost and is now found concentrated in the cells of the reproductive organs.

That the primordial proteins were capable of self-reproduction seems to me personally to be fairly probable, not only for theoretical reasons of the anteriority of the object to its mould, but also because the behaviour of present-day proteins seems to indicate traces of a former capacity for self-reproduction. If one observes the crystallization of proteins and the almost explosive speed at which the crystalline needles multiply in the super-saturated system, one has the definite impression of witnessing a phenomenon of reproduction, though one which, it is true, only brings into play physical and not chemical forces.

The value of the work of Fox's team on the proteinoids is that it enables us to picture one possible form of matter in the prevital state. We can see how matter can, in certain circumstances, conquer a certain number of the characteristic properties of life, and we can guess how the ground was prepared for the equally spontaneous formation of true proteins and living matter capable of reproducing itself.

From all the results provided by biochemical palaeontology, the comparative biochemistry of existing organisms, the ontogenesis of the proteins and the experimental synthesis of the proteinoids, we can conclude, if not with absolute certainty, at least with a high degree of probability, that life issued from matter by a process of spontaneous evolution.

This conclusion is of the highest importance in completing the evolutionary vision of the universe. Teilhard de Chardin had the great merit of clearly bringing out the fundamental importance of the concept of evolution in understanding the meaning of man in the universe. The crucial argument which allowed man to be integrated in the general movement of evolution was the discovery of Java man. It was abundantly confirmed some years later by the Chou kou tien excavations, unearthing the sinanthropoids, and demonstrating with certainty "man's place in nature" as the flower at the topmost of the tree of life.

The views expressed here on prelife and biogenesis show that the tree of life is not only rooted in the earth but that its roots merge with the matter of the earth. The upward continuity of the evolutionary line is now matched by its downward continuity.


## SIGNIFICANCE FOR THE UNDERSTANDING OF EVOLUTION

Having followed science along its various lines of approach to the problem of the origin of life, we must now turn to the second moment of dialectic reflection and look back over the road that has been travelled, but inverting our perspective, so as to discover the inner meaning of this evolutionary movement whose outward manifestation we have been surveying. At this point, what appeared from the external viewpoint of science as a continuity of transformation, reveals itself, viewed from within, as the meaning of the general evolutionary drive of the Universe.

For lack of documentation, *biochemical palaeontology*, provisionally, has so far taught us nothing. From comparative morphology, and more particularly from the *comparative biochemistry* of organisms now living on earth, we learn above all the general uniformity of the structure and properties of living matter, which enables us to assert its unity and to attribute its origin to evolution starting from a single source. From the *morphology of the proteins* as presented to us by biochemistry, we learn the existence of a highly elaborate structuration. The protein, with its remarkable properties, is not these thousands of atoms of carbon, hydrogen and sulphur, but the structure in which they are engaged, their combination in amino acids, the ordered sequence of the polypeptide chain, and finally, the conformation of this chain according to the requirements of secondary, tertiary, and possibly quaternary, structure into an edifice that is as delicate as it is elaborate and capable of the activities of life. Matter lives by the arrangement adopted by the atoms.

This observation gives us a better understanding of the meaning of "complexification" and "concentration". "Complexification" is a term which, if I am not mistaken, was coined by Teilhard and has since come into common use. I must confess to certain hesitations about the use of this neologism, because it is open to ambiguity. One sees what it means, or rather one is too ready to think that one sees: the accumulation of matter has allowed its arrangement in complexes from which a new and superior system has emerged. So far so good. But we should be less ready to agree with someone who allowed himself to be led into associating the idea of "complex" with the idea of the "complicated", the "involved" or the "disordered", since the exact opposite is true. The complexity of the protein is not disorder but supreme order. An orchestral score is complicated to someone who cannot read music, but it would be highly incongruous to call Bach's music complicated. The involved and the indecipherable are only the apparent and completely external side of what is complex. We can only speak of "complexification" so far as it evokes a hierarchy, the appearance of structures and interconnections, the formation of order, and, beyond that, the upsurge of an inner dynamism that is both interiorizing and expansive at the same time. We are bound to confess that this is trying to make the term "complexification" cover a great many things.

To express the same content, the term "concentration" seems preferable; at least it does not look like a neologism, although the meaning which Teilhard gives it is new. But this meaning fits in so well with the word, and the structure of the word so well expresses what it means—the unification of matter around a centre that it reveals, that it creates and that creates itself—that one cannot resist the temptation to prefer it to the other. We may add that the word "concentration" also serves to describe in man the conditions of creation in matter in its highest and most inward form. Artistic creation and scientific discovery only break forth when man has reached a sufficient degree of "concentration" to liberate the spirit.

Reflection on "concentration" leads us to the heart of the subject: *creativity*. This term has not so far been used because it would have required prior definition which we were unable to give. If it is introduced now, it is not because a definition has become possible, but because we can at least refer it to an experience, to a situation that has been experienced, namely "astonishment before the novelty of being springing up out of concentration".

Before going on with our survey, it is worth pausing a moment on the "neologisms" which are so frequent in Teilhard and for which some people so bitterly reproach him. It is not quite true to say that in adopting the term "concentration" rather than that of "complexification" we avoid a neologism. For the term used is only apparently familiar, and in fact we are giving it a new, or at least a wider, meaning. This operation, the exact reverse of a neologism, also has its dangers of ambiguity; the unforewarned reader who takes the word in its habitual meaning remains incapable of grasping the thought, and the word does not help him to discover it. We are in fact faced with a dilemma; to express a vision of the world which is so totally new we are bound to call upon new words or to give old words a new meaning.

The latter solution seems preferable, since it enables us to enrich the language in depth, and the ambiguity is negligible when the new meaning is quite distinct from the original meaning, as in the case of "concentration". There is little danger of confusing "concentration" of matter in evolution with the concentration of a solution or with concentration of mind. But these two meanings are still not foreign to the new one.

But to return to our subject; reflection on the biochemical morphology of the proteins gives us a better understanding of the law of the "concentration" of matter; the accumulation of atoms, their concentration in the physical sense, involves their structuration in higher units, from whence by *concentration*, a new level of being emerges. At the same time, a complete cycle of evolutive "recurrence" is accomplished by the passage through a phase of divergence; the formation of amino acids, their convergence in unordered polypeptides, and finally the emergence of the sequential and structured polypeptide which is the protein.

The biochemistry of proteinic ontogenesis informs us of the extraordinary mechanism of the synthesis of proteins by means of nucleic acids. To explain this mechanism we used the expressions "sentence" and "code", comparing the polypeptide chain to a sentence in which the amino acids played the role of the letters of the alphabet. It will be noted that with its 100 to 200 amino acids, the proteinic chain has the same length as a normal sentence. Similarly, the basic number of proteinic amino acids, and the number of letters of an alphabet, are also of the same order of magnitude—around twenty. We may note in passing that this order of magnitude is universal and essentially linked to the *information* function. Most languages can be expressed by an alphabet of this size. A much shorter alphabet, say of six signs, would not be enough for any language, and much longer it would be redundant.

Over against the alphabet of the amino acids was the code of the nucleic acids. Now the triplets of the nucleotides of the nucleic acids strangely resemble the triplets of the two signs, dot and dash, of the Morse Code, or the perforations in the programme ribbon of a telex system used to transmit an alphabetic message. On reflection, these expressions, sentence, alphabet, code, are more than images or comparisons, they are analogies. Indeed, we must go even further and say that they are analogies in the ontological sense. The same characteristics are found in language and in the protein, because the function is the same—the transmission of information. In other words, there is a participation of being in both cases. And if we admit a relation of information in the sequence of a proteinic polymer in the same way as in a sentence of poetry, we must recognize the presence of the creative spirit in the one as in the other. When all is said and done, one can hardly escape the fact that poetic creation is nothing but a higher concentration of proteinic interactions. The conclusion may seem sacrilege to the poet, but it is poetic for the protein.

The last source of information on the origin of life is the experimental study of biogenesis. The experimental synthesis of the proteinoids, still unfamiliar to the public, is probably destined to startle mankind no less resoundingly than the atomic explosion. But from the point of view of evolution, it nevertheless remains a secondary event, because it results not so much from a primordial force as from an interplay between man and nature.

In spite of its approximations and defects, and even because of them, experimental synthesis reveals the possibilities of life hidden in the atoms. The proteinoids disclose to us the vitality of what we call inert matter. In them we perceive the creative power concealed in the stuff of the universe in evolution. But if we desire to appreciate at its true value the amplitude of this creative power, it is not in the protein-oids that we must look, but at the other extreme of the line, in the man who brings forth these proteinoids in his test-tube. And as the results that emerge from the evolution of matter totally surpass what we can measure and observe in matter, we are led to reverse the perspective, and just as we esteem the letters of a poem only for the poetic inspira-tion that they express, so we are induced to regard the matter of scien-tific experimentation only as the obverse of the creative breath that animates the universe in evolution.


CONCLUSION

In searching for the creative aspects of evolution in the light of Teilhard de Chardin's thought, we started by examining what science teaches us about the transformations of matter which are the origin of life. Reflec-tion on these scientific discoveries then went on to show how this trans-formation revealed a particular aspect of the general evolution of the universe.

The evolution of matter that science observes, measures and tries to reproduce experimentally, and that it seeks to explain, either like Lamarck by the influence of a finality, or following Darwin as the result of mechanical determinisms, appears on reflection to proceed from a process of multiplication and accumulation which engenders a movement of condensation and complexification. Seen from within, this movement takes the form of a concentration which unifies the multiplicity of matter, organizes the diversity of its forces and succeeds in integrating exteriority with such intensity that it emerges in a new state totally surpassing its previous level. Looked at in depth, the con-centration produced in matter reveals itself as the whole movement of evolution, which, charged with the fullness of the past, develops towards the future, but exists only in the actuality of the present, lives in the maturing of its interiority and yields itself up wholly in what it pro-duces. At this level, the true name of concentration is "consciousness", that is to say, the condition of the totality and spontaneity of action, and it becomes legitimate to attribute to matter that supreme property which is, in Bergson's words, a requirement for creation. And along the same line of thought, evolution which has revealed itself to be creative restores to its place of honour an old and highly controversial principle which Pasteur, in spite of polemics, always sought to justify, namely that the origin of life is "spontaneous generation".

# CHAPTER TWO

## Teilhard and the Question of Orthogenesis

by P. G. Fothergill[1]

In a discussion on Teilhard de Chardin on the B.B.C. Television programme *Viewpoint* on 2nd March, 1966, one of the disputants, J. Maynard Smith, a biologist and writer on evolution, perhaps somewhat unnecessarily condemned the ideas of Teilhard de Chardin, particularly because of the latter's views on orthogenesis, which Smith held ran counter to modern genetical teaching. Again, Theodosius Dobzhansky, one of our most accomplished geneticists and evolutionists, supported many of the basic ideas of Teilhard in his book MANKIND EVOLVING,[2] but he rather regretted that Teilhard described evolutionary trends as orthogenetic, although he was sure that by this word Teilhard did not mean that any "uncreative unfolding of preformed events" occurred. Several writers too have asserted that Teilhard's use of orthogenesis was due to his unfamiliarity with modern genetical thought. Verne Grant, a botanist, in THE ORIGIN OF ADAPTATIONS[3] remarked that "there is not a shred of evidence for the theory of orthogenesis in any of its versions". Even the Chairman of this Association, Dr. Bernard Towers, an anatomist, in his small but excellent book called TEILHARD DE CHARDIN[4] considered that Teilhard had really dropped the idea of straight-line evolution, or orthogenesis. Further, a Jesuit philosopher, J. F. Donceel,[5] and also Prof. Maynard Smith, mentioned above, both maintained that orthogenesis is implicit in Teilhard's idea of evolution, and hence his whole system is dependent on it.

Clearly the conclusion would then be that, because orthogenesis is outmoded and discarded by biologists, then Teilhard's ideas are also outmoded. In point of fact, Teilhard himself recognized that his fellow palaeontologists only used the word with disdain and embarrassment.[6]

[1] We regret to record that Dr. Fothergill died on 24 June 1967. Eds.
[2] 1962. (A list of references appears at the end of this chapter.)
[3] 1963, p. 538.
[4] 1966.
[5] 1965, p. 248.
[6] OEUVRES, vol. 3, p. 386.

Yet Teilhard could say in 1955, not long before his death: "Whether it wishes it or not, palaeontology is, and can only become more, *the science of orthogenesis*."[1] Thus, it is clear that there is something wrong here, and all the elements of confusion and misunderstanding are present. In the interests of truth it would seem that this word "orthogenesis" and Teilhard's use of it should be seriously and thoroughly considered. May we then introduce the topic?

An overall view of evolutionary data shows that an undoubted, but not necessarily uninterrupted, movement of matter from a homogeneous to a more heterogeneous state occurs, as Herbert Spencer phrased it, but which is more accurately described as a passage from an unordered to an ordered heterogeneity as Teilhard remarked.[2]

This is a movement from simpler to more complicated; and thus, in the logical and methodological orders, to explain the evolution of "higher" forms from "lower" forms, it became necessary to assume the presence in the evolving organisms of a particular tendency towards progress.[3] It was probably this necessity which first gave the basis and the encouragement to all kinds of orthogenetic ideas in evolution. In 1884, for example, Carl von Nägeli published his MECHANICO-PHYSIO-LOGICAL THEORY OF EVOLUTION. In this theory evolution was visualized as proceeding from simpler to more complex organisms due to indefinable internal urges. At the same time as this striving towards structural perfection occurred there was also a striving towards adaptational perfection. Nägeli did not give any experimental evidence for his theory, but he maintained that it was a rationalistic and mechanistic view of the evolutionary process. Nägeli's views were essentially orthogenetic, and he was probably the first orthogeneticist, although this word was only used later by Haake in 1893.

Another, more empirical, reason for the development of orthogenetic theories was, of course, the discovery of apparently unbroken lines of descent, or evolutionary series, seen among some groups of fossils such as the fossil series of the elephants, the extinct Titanotheres, and the ammonites, etc. It was thought that these fossil series, which showed a kind of determinate straight-line evolution, indicating the existence of trends or directions in evolution, showed a form of development resembling the unrolling of a pattern. Orthogenesis could be

[1] OEUVRES, vol. 3, p. 390.
[2] 1966, p. 33.
[3] See Korschinsky, 1899, p. 273.

likened to a long carpet which as it is unrolled displays the pattern already woven into it. Over the evolutionary scene as a whole ortho-genesis thus presented the evolution of groups of organisms along parallel lines.

The important point of course is what is it that causes the pattern in the carpet? What is it which determines the evolutionary direction? And while there have been many orthogeneticists, many also with their own special views of the process, broadly speaking there are two main opinions as to the cause. Some orthogenetic theories followed the views of Nägeli and postulated the presence of an internal urge inherent in the heredity material or germ plasm. This was imagined as some kind of *élan vital* which works over and above the physico-chemical forces operating in the organism and propels it along its pre-determined path. Other orthogenetic theories found the causal propelling force in the internal or external environment of the organism. This force was considered to be a material factor acting with the physico-chemical forces of the organism to mould it along a certain direction. Further, it was thought to be physiological and there was some evidence to indicate that physiological change preceded structural change, which thus lent weight to orthogenetic theory. Eimer, one of the foremost early orthogeneticists, stated: "I find the actual causes of orthogenesis to lie in the effects of external influences such as climate or nutrition or the constitution of a given organism."[1] But J. S. Huxley denied that there are two chief types of orthogenesis. He considered that there is only one kind—straight-line evolution controlled by an inward directive force.

Nevertheless, very many orthogeneticists have consistently appealed to the external environment as the moulding force governing the evolution of organisms. Thus orthogeneticists are often also Lamarckians. Orthogenesis was also developed to explain some difficult problems which the early selectionists could not solve, such as the persistence of incipient organs before the useful stage was evolved, or the determinate development along fixed lines which in the later stages were not advantageous, or again the fantastic over-development of organs beyond any degree of usefulness. Modern evolutionary theory can, however, give satisfactory explanations of these early difficulties. These modern explanations, while not acknowledging orthogenesis, do not necessarily rule it out when it is taken in a general sense.

[1] See Delage and Goldschmidt, 1912, p. 299.

The real essential point of all orthogenetic theories was that their advocates saw the operation of law in the organic world. They considered that there is a unity in organic nature which does not permit of the operation of indiscriminate forces. Sentiments of this kind were expressed by all the leading orthogeneticists such as Eimer,[1] while Osborn wrote:[2] "As in the domain of inorganic nature, so in the domain of organic nature *fortuity is wanting.*" Berg in 1926, in an interesting book called NOMOGENESIS OR EVOLUTION DETERMINED BY LAW, deliberately adopted this position, and throughout the book he contrasted his ideas and those of other orthogeneticists with the ideas of Darwinists who advocated evolution by means of the natural selection of fortuitous variations. Orthogeneticists did not deny the action of selection, but they considered it to be a conservative rather than a changing force. Berg realized that true straight-line evolution approached the teleological conceptions of Aristotle, but he did not shrink from the implications involved. He countered adverse criticisms by declaring that physics shows us that the phenomena of the physical world are likewise subject to the rule of law which works on them along a definite line. This forced apposition between orthogenesis and Darwinism inevitably led to the discrediting of the former when the modern genetical explanation of selection was begun. But, probably, what was needed was synthesis not apposition.

Often nowadays when a biological writer uses the word orthogenesis he puts it in inverted commas to indicate that he does not quite agree with its use. It is recognized that evolution is the resultant of all the forces operating within and without organisms. This is surely an axiom without which no comprehensive evolutionary theory could even be formulated. Thus, there are probably many causal factors of evolution and there may be some truth in all causal theories advanced up to the present time. The problem, however, is not as simple as we have indicated, and the reader who is interested further may be referred to an excellent review of the subject by Glenn L. Jepsen in a paper given at a symposium on natural selection and adaptation in 1949. Jepsen enumerated many of the reasons why orthogenesis was advocated and why it has largely been rejected. There have been many scientists who have held orthogenetic ideas, but Jepsen pointed out that a survey of the literature showed that orthogenesis has tended to be

[1] 1898.
[2] 1909, p. 225.

c

accepted *as a theory* more by biologists than by palaeontologists, but is accepted *as a descriptive term* for phylogenetic or fossil series more by palaeontologists than by biologists. It will be useful to quote Jepsen in words which sum up the situation.[1] He wrote: "Considering these authors and many others in a recent (and incomplete) census of opinion about orthogenesis, it may be said in summary that, as usual, opinion is divided." And again: "Palaeontology, as known to me, supplies no unequivocal evidence for a theory of orthogenesis or momentum controlled by internal or external drives. The evidence seems rather to support the idea of orthoselection wherein natural selection eliminates certain genetic or biochemical elements and provides the opportunities for others to develop and change and thus, in a sense, to channelize progressive evolution. There are, however, a very great many unanswered questions."

Orthoselection is a term introduced by Plate in 1913. As Jepsen suggested it also gives an explanation in orthodox terms of orthogenetic series or trends in animals. It merely means that, if an adaptive trend exists, selection will lead to improved adaptation provided the environment remains unchanged and the trend continues. Just as in the case of orthogenesis, however, there does not seem to be any direct evidence for orthoselection. It is an attractive and useful idea, as J. S. Huxley considered.[2] But it does not really eliminate orthogenesis as an explanatory or descriptive term, for it presupposes the existence of a trend in an evolutionary series, and this itself still needs an explanation, short of a series of more or less unidirectional and progressive mutations spread over a number of years. Perhaps both orthogenesis and orthoselection are involved in evolutionary series, and Teilhard indeed acknowledged this possibility.

Let us now look at one or two examples of orthogenesis, either true or simulated. First, we may mention the classic example of the evolution of the horse, which has been so often cited as evidence of orthogenesis. Simpson[3] gave a full account of modern and extinct horses. The story of the horse goes back to the beginning of the Eocene period about 60 million years ago. It began with a small creature about the size of a large dog called *Hyracotherium* (or *Eohippus*). At first it was thought that horse fossils showed a true type of straight-line evolution from the

[1] 1949, p. 496.
[2] 1955, p. 500.
[3] 1951.

primitive *Hyracotherium* to *Equus*, the modern horse. But further study and more numerous fossils (and a very large number have been found) showed that the evolutionary development of the horse resembles a bush rather than a straight line or even a series of straight lines. *Hyracotherium* did not mutate successively and in one direction only, as it were, to give the horse ultimately and with no interruption in the sequence. There have in fact been many genera and species of horses, some closely and some distantly connected to *Equus*. On the other hand, all of the creatures in these fossil lineages of horse-like animals have probably arisen ultimately from *Hyracotherium*, that is, *Hyracotherium* is the common ancestor of all of them. If there is any basis in the general assumption of evolution itself that fossils provide evidence for the process, then presumably the horse fossils show a general movement from the common ancestor to *Equus*.

The direct ancestors of the modern horse as we know it today, are usually stated as firstly, *Hyracotherium* in the lower Eocene Period, secondly *Orohippus*, and next *Epihippus* in the late Eocene Period. Then we proceed through the Oligocene Period with *Mesohippus* and *Miohippus*, next the Miocene Period with the horses *Parahippus* and *Merychippus*, and finally we encounter *Pliohippus* in the more recent Pliocene Period before we arrive at *Equus*. If this evolutionary series or trend has any real evolutionary meaning, it implies that all these creatures are more or less remotely but truly genetically connected, that is, that one is descended from the other but not necessarily in straight-line fashion. Indeed, Professor Simpson[1] has detailed the possible course of this evolutionary process in terms of mutations. Since *Hyracotherium* lived in the lower Eocene Period, Simpson calculated that there must have been at least 15 million generations involving some 1,500 billion individuals in all stages of the evolutionary sequence. During this evolution, slow but characteristic changes occurred from the small teeth of *Hyracotherium* to the large grinding teeth of the modern horse. Supposing each change of tooth character had been controlled by one gene, then over the 60 million years involved, at least $1\frac{1}{2}$ million mutations would have occurred on the chromosome concerned in the process. Simpson considered that if only one-thousandth of these mutations had been effective, they would account for the evolution of the horse teeth. Simpson, however, did not consider that this evolution shows orthogenesis, and indeed it does not

[1] 1961, pp. 109–110.

show straight-line evolution without any deviations. Nevertheless, in the logical and descriptive orders it can scarcely be denied that there has been a true and progressive evolution from "simpler", less complex, to "advanced", more complex, and evolved horse-like organisms. The term orthogenesis has been used, and may surely still be used, to cover this type of undoubtedly directional series of changes whether actually continuous or not. And this use of the word does not imply the operation of any mystical forces. In any case the forces controlling the process occurred so long ago, and are unknown, except by inferences from genetical and evolutionary principles, which themselves are inferences from similar past and present occurrences. Again, there is no direct experimental evidence for orthogenesis, and there cannot be; neither is there any direct evidence in this sense for evolution itself.

From a large-scale example such as the one we have just given let us pass to a small-scale biochemical example. Histidine is an amino acid which is of great importance in the biosynthesis of the protein histone, which itself is very important to the regulatory mechanisms involved in cell metabolism. Histidine is synthesized by the cell from two substances called adenosine triphosphate and phosphoribosyl-pyrophosphate in the presence of magnesium. The details of this synthesis have been worked out for the organism *Salmonella*,[1] and it involves the production of ten intermediate substances which must be formed in a fixed and definite order. Each step in the synthesis is under the control of a different gene, except for two genes which each control two different steps. Thus there are 11 steps controlled by 9 genes in this synthesis. The genes involved, of course, while different are all thought to be borne on the same *Salmonella* chromosome, but at different loci or positions. Thus, the evolution of the histidine synthesis does not show a straight-line evolution. But nevertheless, and inasmuch as the intermediate substances produced in the synthesis are of use only as precursors in the production of the following substance produced in the cycle, then this evolution has clearly been unidirectional in the production of an essential protein. Once again the evolution of such a cycle may be described as orthogenetic without any implications of mysterious causal agencies; the cycle consists of a movement in a certain and inevitable direction which only becomes evident after the process has evolved and which finds its justification in the end-product.

In a very short survey we have attempted to give an account of

[1] See an account in Hartman and Suskind, 1965, pp. 574, 78–79.

some of the meanings of orthogenesis as used in biology and palaeontology. We have seen that, in general, the concept is mostly rejected because of the association of the word with some teleological, or mystical forces which were supposed to be its cause. But in general terms opinion about orthogenesis remains divided. Further, and what is probably more important from the scientific point of view, there is no experimental evidence for straight-line evolution. The known facts of modern genetical and evolutionary studies, and a greater understanding of palaeontology, coupled with the larger numbers of available fossils, indicate that the evidence from the mutatio-selection theory are sufficient to account for the evolutionary trends which gave rise to the theory of orthogenesis. Evolution is a discontinuous process at the lower operative levels where change actually occurs; it is also irreversible in general, but not completely so. Thus modern evolutionists are correct in rejecting those aspects of orthogenesis which appeal to unknown urges, etc. On the other hand, it is only correct to notice also that the word has an etymological meaning implying the presence of an overall sense or inclination of direction in evolution. While strict straight-line evolution, and evolution propelled by internal urges are undoubtedly false ideas, evolution in general and evolutionary series large or small, in particular, also show a general progression in certain directions—a goal is always reached in spite of reversals which are sometimes encountered. It may thus be said that, while evolution consists of a series of discontinuities, the process operates in a stream of overall continuity and is orthogenetic in this context. It is the etymological meaning of orthogenesis which has distinct logical, methodological and descriptive applications in biology and palaeontology which could be recognized, and which indeed to some minds at least seem obvious applications.

Orthogenesis in this etymological sense seemed clear to Teilhard de Chardin. He recognized the dangers of being misunderstood in using the word, but he pointed out that it is possible to correct the use of the word rather than to reject it completely, and so he appealed for its retention in biology and palaeontology. This attitude, of course, was in keeping with the logic of his thought and the development of his ideas. He struggled hard to convince his fellow scientists that it is urgently necessary for them to consider consciousness as an integral part of things, that is, to consider the "within" on equal terms with the "without". He struggled hard to convince scientists that they are entitled to give a whole explanation of phenomena not just one based solely on empirical data. And so, in his application of orthogenesis to his observed facts, he strived to show, or to indicate, that inferences drawn from assembled observational data, but which are more philosophical than empirical, are still nevertheless necessary and valid in order to understand the process of evolution as a whole. Indeed, Teilhard's law of complexity-consciousness, which is basic to his whole system, and also much of the evidence for the occurrence of evolution itself, is dependent on reasoning of this kind. Teilhard, therefore, in defending his use of orthogenesis was not initiating anything new.

We should now examine some of Teilhard's statements about orthogenesis. In just two of his books, THE PHENOMENON OF MAN and THE APPEARANCE OF MAN, Teilhard used the word orthogenesis, and gave accounts of what he meant by it, at least two dozen times. Clearly he attached importance to his meaning of orthogenesis, so much so that in 1955, shortly before he died, he prepared a paper on the 'Defence of Orthogenesis' which was later published in LA VISION DU PASSÉ.[1] Let us be clear from the beginning that Teilhard did not propose any *theory* of orthogenesis, that is, a complete system of evolutionary causation based on orthogenesis. Indeed, he did not regard orthogenesis in a causal sense at all. To him orthogenesis was a kind of evolutionary quality which became evident through consideration of evolutionary lines, resulting from the operation of the accepted causal factors such as mutation, selection, recombination, etc. Even as evolution is the resultant of all these factors, orthogenesis to Teilhard was thus merely the extension in a theoretical sense of this resultant. Theoretical, but still important and necessary to an understanding of evolution. We may express this point in another way. Just as evolution is a general conclusion and is not measurable (we can only measure mutation rates, etc.), so also orthogenesis is a conclusion drawn from evolutionary data and which also is not measurable, but which gives a qualitative aspect to the evolutionary process, and perhaps allows further more far-reaching conclusions to be drawn by extrapolation.

In THE PHYLETIC STRUCTURE OF THE HUMAN GROUP[2] Teilhard was careful to point out that the phenomena of mutation and orthogenesis should not be "contrasted as irreconcilables". Mutations, of course, are recognized as the actual changes, or building blocks, of evolution. As

[1] OEUVRES, vol. 3, 1957.
[2] ANN. PALAEONTOL. **37**, 1951, and THE APPEARANCE OF MAN, 1965.

far as we know they are chiefly random occurrences, but Teilhard pointed out that there is no contradiction between the play of chance shown by the random appearance of mutations and the existence of any fundamental preferences in the objects mutating. On the contrary, the association of chance and orientation are necessary aspects of life which connect the short-term and the long-term features of hierarchic evolutionary structures.

Teilhard maintained all evolutionists acknowledge that living matter speciates forming lines, radiations or trends and producing the various phyla, or groups, that we know over vast periods of time, and further, that within these larger groups other transformations occur. Evolution is thus progressive and divergent, but Teilhard considered that it is also a process of intensification in the additive development of this or that character prolonged continuously and indefinitely. Intensification is thus oriented. Historically and palaeontologically we call the results of this process "phylogeny", and we have some extensive knowledge of the way in which phylogenesis works at the micro-level of genetics. But Teilhard still maintained that there is a gap, a lack of connection, between the phylogeny of the palaeontologists and the genetics of speciation. He considered that phylogeny could be more completely harmonized with known evolutionary laws if palaeontologists would only recognize that evolution on the phylogenetic level shows a direction, an orientation, that is, if they would acknowledge at least a descriptive and methodological orthogenesis.

In THE PHENOMENON OF MAN[1] Teilhard wrote: "There seems to be no lack of examples, in the course of biological evolution, of transformations acting horizontally by pure crossing of characters. One example is the mutation we call Mendelian. But when we look deeper and more generally we see the rejuvenations made, possible by each reproduction, achieve something more than mere restitution. They add, one to the other, and their sum increases *in a pre-determined direction*. Dispositions are accentuated, organs are adjusted or supplemented. We get diversification, the growing specialization of factors forming a single genealogical sequence—in other words, the appearance of the *line* as a natural unit distinct from the *individual*. This law of controlled complication, the mature stage of the process in which we first get the micro-molecule then the mega-molecule and finally the first cells, is known to biologists as *orthogenesis*. . . . Orthogenesis is the only com-

[1] 1959, pp. 108–109.

plete form of heredity. The word conceals deep and real springs of cosmic extent. . . . Thanks to its characteristic additive power, living matter (unlike the matter of the physicists) finds itself 'ballasted' with complications and instability. It falls, or rather rises, towards forms that are more and more improbable. . . . Without orthogenesis life would only have spread; with it there is an ascent of life that is invincible."

In the above words Teilhard put forth his overall general meaning of orthogenesis in the widest possible sense. He also gave more precise meaning to it in several places, for example, when he described it etymologically as meaning oriented development giving rise to a "vectorial" quality. Without this vectorial quality one could not speak of trends, or even of phyla, and in this sense, orthogenesis does not imply any idea of monophyletism or of finality, at least to begin with.[1] He described orthogenesis in another way by saying that it shows a clearcut property of living matter to "form a system in which terms succeed each other experimentally, following the constantly increasing values of centro-complexity".[2]

The last description given above connects orthogenesis to Teilhard's fundamental law of complexity-consciousness. According to Teilhard an examination of the evolutionary process as a whole shows two main features which occur at both the micro- and the macro-levels. These features are: (a) an increasing complexification of forms from the earliest to the latest (or from the "lowest" to the "highest"), and (b) an increase in consciousness also from the earliest to the latest. These two features are so constant, so interwoven and so fundamental in evolution, that evolution may be said to be only the manifestation of a law of increasing complexity-consciousness. This law, according to Teilhard, whereby matter if left to itself over a long period of time inevitably develops along lines of increasing improbability, is as fundamental in biology as any of the great physical laws. The operation of this law throughout evolution from the simplest atomic particle up to the highest animal, manifests a clear general trend, the direction which evolution could only take, and its best effects are most distinctly seen in the evolution and development of nervous tissue in higher animals. As Teilhard wrote: "Among the infinite modalities in which the complication of life is dispersed, the differentiation of nervous tissue stands out,

[1] 1965, THE APPEARANCE OF MAN, p. 215.
[2] 1959, THE PHENOMENON OF MAN, p. 108.

as theory would lead us to expect, as a significant transformation. *It provides a direction;* and by its consequences *it proves that evolution has a direction.*"[1] Thus the law of complexity-consciousness provides the first and basic manifestation of orthogenesis from which all variations of the phenomenon spring.

Teilhard recognized two main kinds of orthogenesis,[2] and unfortunately he used different words to describe them as follows:

(a) *Orthogénèse de fond:* here the word orthogenesis is used in a phenomenological sense to describe the general orthogenesis of the whole biosphere. This is the primary or general drift shown by matter in its movement towards greater complexity and towards greater consciousness or interiorization. It is most clearly expressed in the increasing concentration of nervous tissues in animals. Teilhard also called this a "general orthogenesis of corpusculization", "mega-orthogenesis" and "basic orthogenesis".

(b) *Orthogénèse de forme:* here the word is used in a biological sense to emphasize what Teilhard considered to be secondary or under-drifts. This is the orthogenesis of speciation in all its forms. He also called it "micro-orthogenesis" or a "section of orthogenesis in miniature", as in the example of the Australopiths or Southern Ape-men. In this speciating orthogenesis evolution is visualized as proceeding through an incredible number of different forms, and through a series of small changes, pushing out in all directions, but acted on by natural selection, which, in the end, provides the course and gives rise to the various evolutionary lines, trends or radiations, etc. In a word, micro-orthogenesis is the orthogenesis of differentiation within the phyla, or large groups of organisms like phyla.

Within these two major types of orthogenesis Teilhard was quite open in his attitude towards the basic causes of the whole process. In general he considered orthogenesis to act under two main types of cause, and to describe them he used the words *orthoselection* and *ortho-election.* These are not neologisms. We have already mentioned that selectionists have used the term "orthoselection" in an effort to describe orthogenetic phenomena, and, as with selectionists, Teilhard also used the word to indicate that type of orthogenesis where the selective influence of the environment dominated the evolutionary direction taken by the organism concerned. This is obviously the usual Darwinian

[1] 1959, p. 146.
[2] See also Cuénot, 1963, pp. 64–65.

mutatio-selection view of evolutionary causation. But Teilhard also showed certain leanings towards some limited kind of Lamarckism, and he used "orthoelection" to describe this type of orthogenesis, in which the conscious or unconscious inventive capacity of life dominated the evolutionary trend. Orthoelection, of course, is most clearly seen in man.

Thus Teilhard superimposed his ideas of orthogenesis on to the usual causal explanations of evolution, such as natural selection. He was not substituting a theory of selection by one of orthogenesis, and in spite of what some writers have said to the contrary, he allowed for the full play in evolution of all the other factors recognized by biologists, but to which he added a rather vague environmental factor for which he had no real evidence. Teilhard in fact considered evolution to be a statistical result of the play of large numbers in a general movement of matter. For example, in THE PHENOMENON OF MAN, when discussing ways of life, he wrote: "Life advances by mass effects, by dint of multitudes flung into action without apparent plan. Milliards of germs and millions of adult growths, jostling, shoving and devouring one another, fight for elbow room and for the best and largest living space." And he continued: "But it is not the individual unit that seems to count for most in the phenomenon. What we find within the struggle to live is something deeper than a series of duels; it is a conflict of chances. By reckless self-reproduction life takes its precautions against mishap. It increases its chances of survival and at the same time multiplies its chances of progress."[1]

Nature proliferates profusely, she reproduces almost recklessly, but she also differentiates and intensifies. This is the way of evolution; the way in which organisms, having once attained life, continue it and seek out, in a variety of circumstances, to expand themselves and their descendants. Evolution is divergent. Teilhard emphasized that, both in its individuals and in its speciating mechanisms, evolutionary units are submitted to processes of trial and error on the grand scale. It is as though evolutionary nature is continually experimenting with its units. And so Teilhard was brought to recognize another fundamental feature of nature, which is a direct result of the play of statistically large numbers; this is the phenomenon, or technique, of *groping*. Groping is the specific weapon of all expanding multitudes. As Teilhard said: "This groping strangely combines the blind fantasy of large numbers

[1] 1959, pp. 109–110.

with the precise orientation of a specific target. It would be a mistake
to see it as mere chance. Groping is *directed chance*. It means pervading
everything, and trying everything so as to find everything."[1]

Teilhard attached as much importance to this technique of groping
as he did to that of orthogenesis. At first sight groping would seem to
stand in contradiction to orthogenesis, but examination shows that
such is not the case, just as examination also shows that Teilhard's
view of orthogenesis is not anti-selectionist. Indeed, groping is a
phenomenon seen at the micro-level of evolution where natural selection and mutations can be seen to act directly. And it is the very
random nature of these processes, the uncertainties of mutation and the
"luck" of selection, operating on large numbers of organisms, which
cause the groping. Groping is thus the manifestation of mutation combined with selection, but it is evident only when one considers their
combined action from the outside as it were and in statistically significant quantities. Teilhard wrote: "If life has been able to advance it is
because, by ceaseless groping, it has successively found points of least
resistance at which reality yielded to its thrust."[2]

We may say that it is Teilhard's emphasis on groping which
validates his use of orthogenesis. It is by life pushing forward in various
directions that, having found a new mutation or a new compartment,
it can enter in and continue pushing forward in its turn and so on indefinitely. Evolution is thus not a mere continuous spreading-out
reaching nowhere, because trial and error, or groping, ensure that life
finds its direction. Evolution is a dialectic between emergence and
divergence and, at certain levels, of convergence also. Chance and
direction, groping and orthogenesis, are essential, overall and subsidiary
features of this dialectic. We see then that there is nothing "mystical",
no internal urges, nothing mysterious, about Teilhard's idea of orthogenesis. He uses the idea in fact in a legitimate sense which arises from
a general consideration of evolutionary phenomena and from more
detailed consideration of evolutionary lines. Teilhard's orthogenesis is
not a theory of evolutionary causation, as we have emphasized. It is
really a plea which he makes to his fellow scientists to recognize that
evolution, like all natural processes, is a law-abiding process and manifests direction; it is not a chaotic and useless process. Orthogenesis to Teilhard seems to be the means whereby mechanistic evolu-

[1] 1959, p. 110.
[2] 1959, p. 280.

tion can become expanded into a satisfactory evolutionism, and this is the reason why one may say that orthogenesis is important to Teilhard's system of thought.

Teilhard's view of orthogenesis is very similar to what C. H. Waddington[1] in a recent Riddell Memorial Lecture called a chreodic system. A *chreod* is a pathway in a definite direction; it is an obligatory pathway rendered necessary by the active constituents of a (biological) system. The mere presence of certain inherent constituents in such systems determines the direction in which the system moves. It is seen excellently in the development of human and animal organisms, but it is not confined to the biological sphere. It may, for example, be seen in the operation of computers or in guided aeroplanes and the like. Chreodic systems clearly have a large part to play in determining the course of evolution and in this respect there would seem to be little difference between Teilhard's phenomena of orthogenesis and groping and Waddington's chreodic systems. Such systems are self-stabilizing, and Waddington asserts that in many ways they resemble unconscious purposive mechanisms. Given further evolutionary developments such as that of reflection in man, chreodic systems may be joined to the conscious purpose of man, thus helping to provide a place for purpose and teleology in an otherwise purely empirical biology.

However, the fact remains that all known evolutionary occurrences can be explained satisfactorily in purely empirical terms following accepted scientific laws. To give a scientific, biological or genetical account of any parts of the evolutionary process it is not necessary to consider orthogenesis, even in Teilhard's sense. It is, of course, implied in the frequent use of terms such as trends or adaptive radiations, but its use here is mostly descriptive. Directed evolution is not, strictly speaking, measurable; it is really one of those conclusions or inferences on the border-line of science and philosophy, which we draw from the observed data taken as a whole. It only enters into evolutionary considerations if one wishes to give a total explanation of the meaning of evolution. Teilhard was, of course, quite aware of this problem, but then the object of his whole synthesis was to seek a total explanation in all-embracing terms. He sought to bring the scientist and the philosopher closer together. By Teilhard's insistence on the importance of the basic law of complexity-consciousness and on the importance of dealing with the "within", it may be maintained that he has made it possible for

[1] 1966.

orthogenesis and similar ideas to be dealt with at the scientific level.

J. F. Donceel in an excellent paper called 'Teilhard de Chardin: scientist or philosopher'[1] has dealt with some of the problems raised by this issue. Donceel considered that in the final analysis, the scientist, whether he wishes it or not, and whether he acknowledges it or not, if he endeavours to give a total explanation of his phenomena, must also philosophize. As far as evolution is concerned, the reconciliation between the problems which Teilhard raised by his insistence on orthogenesis may be solved by recognizing that there are two levels of causality in evolution—the phenomenal and the nomenal, efficient and formal causality, or in Teilhard's own terms, the tangential and the radial levels. These levels are complementary to each other, and Teilhard would maintain that they become merged ultimately, on the basis that causality itself is a manifestation of energy. Of course, we have reached the old problem of whether a scientist can also be a philosopher at the same time and *vice versa*, or whether the two must be kept rigidly apart. Here one must make one's own choice. As far as the scientist is concerned, in the phenomenal empirical field no choice is needed, he can pursue his science at the scientific level alone. But if he wishes to develop a synthesis of reality such as Teilhard envisaged, he must deal with both the empirical and the intelligible aspects of things. In fact, Teilhard has not by any means been the only scientist to seek a total explanation, and who was able to reconcile methodological conflicts within himself. In truth, a person *is* one within himself, and is perfectly capable of seeking a unified explanation of the reality of which he is a part.

## REFERENCES

BERG, L. S., 1926. *Nomogenesis or Evolution determined by Law*, trans. by T. J. McCormack, Chicago.

CUÉNOT, C., 1963. *Lexique Teilhard de Chardin*, Paris.

DELAGE, Y. & GOLDSCHMIDT, M., 1962. *The Theories of Organic Evolution*, London.

DOBZHANSKY, T., 1962. *Mankind Evolving*, London.

DONCEEL, J. F., 1965. Teilhard de Chardin: Scientist or Philosopher, *Int. Philos. Quat.* **5**, No. 2, 248.

EIMER, T., 1898. *On Orthogenesis and the Importance of Natural Selection in Species Formation*, trans. by T. J. McCormack, Chicago.

GRANT, VERNE, 1963. *The Origin of Adaptations*, London.

[1] 1965.

HARTMAN, P. E. & SUSKIND, S. R., 1965. *Gene Action*, London.
HUXLEY, J. S., 1955. *Evolution: the Modern Synthesis*, London.
JEPSEN, GLENN L., 1949. Selection, 'Orthogenesis', and the fossil record, *Proc. Amer. Philos. Soc.*, **93**, No. 6, 479.
KORSCHINSKY, S., 1899. Heterogenesis and Evolution, *Naturw. Wschr.* **14**, 273, and in *Flora*, **89**, 1901.
OSBORN, H. F., 1909. *Darwin and Palaeontology, Fifty Years of Darwinism*, New York.
SIMPSON, G. G., 1951. *Horses*, Oxford.
SIMPSON, G. G., 1961. *The Major Features of Evolution*, 3rd impr. Columbia.
TEILHARD DE CHARDIN, P., 1951. The phyletic structure of the human group, *Ann. Palaeontol.* **37**.
TEILHARD DE CHARDIN, P., 1957. *La Vision Du Passé*, Paris.
TEILHARD DE CHARDIN, P., 1959, *The Phenomenon of Man*, London.
TEILHARD DE CHARDIN, P., 1965. *The Appearance of Man*, London.
TEILHARD DE CHARDIN, P., 1966. *Man's Place in Nature*, London.
WADDINGTON, C. H., *Biology and Human Purpose*, 38th Riddell Memorial Lectures, University of Newcastle upon Tyne, November 28th–30th, 1966.

# CHAPTER THREE

## Human Embryology and the Law of Complexity-Consciousness

by Bernard Towers

It is reasonable to suppose that the problem of his origin is one that has intrigued man ever since he became capable of self-reflection. The question of group-origin (phylogeny) seems to have interested primitive man more than that of individual origin (ontogeny), a point which is significant for the analogies we shall be making between the two types of "development". But the latter, which constitutes the subject of embryology, must also have caused man to wonder from his early days. It is not without significance that small children go through a period of intense curiosity (which is not at all prurient) on the subject of where babies come from. The myths and lies that their enquiries have so often elicited in recent centuries represent one aspect of the failure of Western civilization, and Christianity in particular, to respect an honest search for truth and its normal means of communication through natural phenomena. If one does not respect honest enquiry, then distortion of truth is inevitable. Anyone who looks through distorted spectacles for any length of time is likely to have his vision permanently affected. Amongst adults today, including many, of course, who are themselves fathers and mothers, there is astonishing ignorance of some of the basic facts concerning human embryological development. Errors of interpretation abound. One does not expect everyone to become an embryologist, but he ought at least to be informed about some of the fundamental conclusions of this branch of medical science.

The subject is not the easiest to study or to comprehend. Like all the biological sciences, but to a greater degree than many of them, it is complicated by the fact that the time-dimension is of crucial importance. Most things in nature are difficult enough to analyse even when they stand still (in so far as anything in nature ever does stand still). But when there are whole series of inbuilt and progressive changes occurring in living-organisms along a time-axis whose intervals are comparatively brief, then they become very difficult to handle conceptually. Our thought-processes tend to have a great inertia about them. This is perhaps because we experience ourselves as somewhat static creatures, and after all it is we who engage in thought-processes. We feel, know ourselves to be, today, very much the same as we were yesterday, and as we expect to be tomorrow. The pace of life, and our appreciation of the speed of change, may vary according to the particular period through which we happen to be living at the moment, and to the degree of interest (or lack of it) and happiness (or lack of it) that we are currently enjoying. But most people recognize no great change in themselves from day to day, or even from year to year. We must all have had that curious experience of meeting a group of acquaintances from the past, and being struck by how much more *they* all have changed than we have ourselves.

Now an embryo is unable, or so it would seem, to reflect upon itself in these terms, and on the developmental changes it undergoes. But if it could, it would see more change in itself in a day than we see in ourselves in a decade. Later I shall outline the type and speed of change that occur. For the moment let us merely reflect that if all life can be legitimately thought of as a journey towards death, there can be no doubt that the speed of travel measured in biological time, that is by the speed of biological change, is fastest in the embryo. Subsequently there is a gradual deceleration unless and until one of a small group of illnesses overtakes one. The embryo, as a professional colleague of mine once observed, rushes headlong not merely towards independent life but also towards the grave. It is perhaps as well we don't keep up that pace.

This was all by way of introduction to the difficulties inherent in what is pre-eminently a four-dimensional study. The key to modern understanding of natural phenomena lies in the proper appreciation of the dimension of time. We know now, from our recognition of the evolutionary process, that time is not merely one more component of the static or the cyclical. But Western European culture developed for over two millenia with the notion that time, like length and breadth and depth, could be divided up indefinitely into smaller and smaller portions. The concept of the "atom" or "that which cannot be divided", was as much a puzzle for our forbears as are subatomic particles to the average man today. Scholars used to toy with the notion that if one only thought about it logically enough one would see that an arrow shot from its bow ought never to reach its target because of the indefinitely divisible nature of both space and time. The notion is clearly fallacious, but it is difficult to fault it logically on traditional Western premises about the nature of things. As a professional anatomist I might perhaps be allowed to say that, much as I value the detailed knowledge that has resulted from our anatomizing and analysing (literally cutting up and loosening up) everything we come across, yet one result of the habit is much to be regretted: as small boys quickly learn, it is much easier to take things to pieces than to put them back together again. Performing an anatomy or analysis is only the first step towards understanding. Nothing is fully understandable except it is seen in its wholeness, and any individual part makes ultimate sense only in the relation it bears to the whole.

It is a somewhat unnerving experience to browse around in the field of the History of Embryology (as you may do, for instance, in Dr. Joseph Needham's classic book of that title).[1] For all man's natural interest in the processes of generation, and discounting the occasional insights of men of genius, the truth is that until as recently as a hundred years ago (that is, well into the Scientific Age) the most absurd errors in observation, and crass misinterpretations, were still being made concerning embryos. Of course it is only comparatively recently that biology emerged from the status of a branch of natural history to become one of the natural sciences. This was when it acquired, and finally accepted after many battles, the unifying and stimulating Darwinian hypothesis of Evolution. One can still read with profit pre-evolutionary works in some branches of biology. In the works of Richard Owen, say, or in the lectures of John Hunter, one marvels at the range of knowledge displayed, and at the acuteness and accuracy of the observations they made. But what is one to say of their contemporaries amongst embryologists who, long after the discovery of the microscope (the lack of which might be held to excuse earlier workers) were divided into two such incompatible groups as the so-called Ovists and Animalculists? The first group held that the embryo was entirely the product of the maternal egg, for which the male provided only a stimulus. The second group saw, or thought they saw down the microscope, a complete miniature human being in every spermatozoon, awaiting only the fertile soil of the womb to become animated and start to grow. This idea of the nature and power of the male seed is, of course, a very ancient one. It probably provided the basis for one rationalization of ancient conquering tribes. They would

[1] 1934 (2nd Edition 1959), C.U.P.

D

slaughter the male members of the defeated group, in order to prevent admixture of foreign blood, but would take the females into captivity and breed with them. Although the mother of a child clearly had an influence on her baby before as well as after birth, it was believed that the practice did not put into jeopardy the purity of the race, because it was only the male seed that was thought to give rise to the offspring itself. The Animalculists were their natural successors in a scientific milieu. By contrast, the Ovists were out-and-out feminists. One doubts if anyone holds such views as either of these today, but others equally erroneous are clearly present in the popular imagination.

I speak of these things not for the sake of recounting items of folk-lore and myth, but to emphasize the point that modern understanding of embryological development is of very recent origin, and as yet we have only scratched the surface of the subject. Doubtless we are today still making faulty observations, and drawing faulty conclusions. One only hopes that our descendants will recognize them as honest errors, such as were made in this field by the great William Harvey. He might well have made embryological discoveries that subsequently lay hidden for two hundred years more, if he had not chanced, because of the opportunities afforded him during the Royal Hunts, to investigate early mammalian development in deer, one species of which has the curious trick of holding the fertilized ovum in a state of suspended animation for weeks after breeding, before embryological development begins. Harvey was quite misled as a result. Other honest errors of interpretation, made by earlier scientists, include that of the fact that sometimes a hen's egg, immediately after laying, can be seen down the microscope to have a minute but distinct embryological form within it. This fact, together with the observation that hens lay fertile eggs for up to three weeks after mating, provided strong arguments for the Ovists, who held that the function of the male was simply to provide a "fecundating influence" on the female, who then produced fertile eggs for as long as the influence persisted. The occasional, and valid, observation of some kind of embryological form immediately after the egg was laid made them at one with the Animalculists in accepting "preformation" as against the alternative hypothesis of "epigenesis" in embryological development. Their errors stem from the fact that they were not to know how long avian spermatozoa from a single ejaculation can survive to fertilize a succession of eggs. Nor did they know how many hours some-times a fertilized egg will remain in the oviduct before laying, thus allowing for development of recognizable embryological form prior to its accessibility for investigation. These are, therefore, what I call honest errors, such as are recognized as part and parcel of scientific life. They are always corrigible. Their correction depends not only on improved observation, but also on a readiness, which is basic to all true scientists, though not, of course, invariably practised, to recognize mistakes and to lose no time in rectifying them.

It is not so easy to forgive the other major source of the many errors in the history of human embryology. Few sciences have been so bedevilled by ignorant, unwarranted speculation. By this I mean the application of metaphysical or theological principles or beliefs to natural phenomena prior to their objective examination simply as phenomena. Or, alternatively, the acceptance of one scientific hypothesis and the rejection of another because of philosophical or theological predilections, and the subsequent incorporation of the preferred *schema* into some kind of theological orthodoxy. The church's position on the nature of sex and the ethics of contraception would have been different if corrigible scientific hypotheses had not been so affected, one way or another, by authoritarian theological considerations. Theological premises must never be allowed to predetermine what is to be admissible as evidence concerning natural phenomena. Theology is still queen of the sciences, but she must learn to behave as a constitutional monarch and not an autocrat. If theologians wish to speculate about the status of the embryo they should first learn some embryology at first hand in the laboratory. So too, of course, should politicians who wish to legislate for destruction of embryos by artificial abortion. In the seventeenth and eighteenth centuries theological fashion insisted that those who taught the Aristotelian theory of epigenesis, that is that an embryo undergoes gradual development involving changes of shape and increasing complexity of organization, were little better than atheists. The preformation theory was preferred, and is perhaps the reason for the popularity in sophisticated circles of the "homunculus", as the mythical little man in the spermatozoon was called. Not all of these errors are of the honest kind. This is an ever-present danger, against which we must always be on our guard.

Real advances in embryological knowledge came in the second half of the nineteenth century. In view of the enormous interest during the same period in evolutionary theory, it is not surprising that parallels were drawn between ontogenetic and phylogenetic development. There are, indeed, many interesting and wholly valid analogies to be drawn. Embryology provides some of the strongest direct evidence there is in favour of the general concept of evolution. But in the first flush of nineteenth-century enthusiasm speculation undoubtedly went much too far in this direction. If a prior theological or philosophical conviction can distort one's appreciation and understanding of natural phenomena, so too can a strongly held scientific belief. The results of such distortion are always inhibiting, and can hold back progress in the subject for years or decades. Scientists in the late nineteenth century summed up their beliefs about the relationship between evolution and embryology in the phrase "ontogeny recapitulates phylogeny". A more popular, that is less technical, expression was that the embryo climbs up its own evolutionary tree during the course of its development. Similar expressions, or at least their implications, are still to be found in popular books and magazine articles. In so far as the general public is aware of anything very much concerning the embryo, these are some of the ideas that seem today to permeate our culture. The most facile arguments were and still are advanced in support of the notion that in its early stages of development a human embryo is "nothing but" a kind of amoeba or a minute mass of vegetable matter; or that later, when it is seen, at about three weeks of development, to have a long thin body (measured, of course, in millimetres only), and is segmented like a worm, that it really is "nothing but" a worm-like invertebrate. At four and five weeks one sees the so-called "gill-arches" and "gill-clefts" that have led superficial observers to conclude that this really is a fish-stage, that human embryos go through a period as fishes swimming in their private intra-uterine pond. Then there is the time when the developing nervous system, and the vertebral column that houses it, outstrips the development of the rest of the trunk. This leads to the transient appearance of a tail on the embryo. It has been argued, then, that this represents a true monkey-stage in human development. So too the appearance of the first-formed body-hair, which is longer than the "down" to which we are more accustomed, and which is shed before birth normally, has been cited as evidence of a non-human stage in development.

All these facts—and the observed phenomena must be regarded as facts in a strict sense—provide powerful evidence, as mentioned earlier, in support of the general theory of evolution, and of the kinship that undoubtedly exists not only between different races of men, but also between man and the rest of nature. But simply to conclude that "ontogeny recapitulates phylogeny" is to ignore another whole empire of scientific knowledge, namely the science of genetics.

We now know enough about heredity, and the way that genetic information is coded in linear fashion on the chromosomes of the nucleus of every cell in our bodies, to be able to state categorically that the recapitulation-theory, in the form it took in the past, was false. That is not to say it was not a useful theory. One of the principal functions of scientific theories is to stimulate thoughtful enquiry, and this the recapitulation-theory certainly did. The element of truth that it contained has been most clearly expounded by Sir Gavin de Beer, whose book EMBRYOS AND ANCESTORS[1] finally demolished its nineteenth-century formulation. De Beer concludes that embryos do not successively resemble, and cannot legitimately be homologized with, the *adult* forms of their evolutionary ancestors. But embryos do resemble ancestral *embryonic* forms. This fact can provide many valuable leads in working out phylogenetic relations. But knowledge of genetics precludes our ever stating that an embryo of one species is "nothing but" an example of some simpler, more primitive form. That cannot be, because the pattern of the chromosomes, which determine the developmental potential, and direct the actual development, of the growing creature, is quite specific and precise. Each one of us inherited, from the time when our mother's egg was fertilized by our father's sperm, not only all our shared characteristics but also many of those that are quite individual, such as the precise colour of our eyes and skin, our fingerprints and the shape of our faces. So far as shared hereditable characteristics are concerned, it is because of them that we are members of the genus *Homo* and of the order *Primata*, members of the class *Mammalia* and of the sub-phylum *Vertebrata*. Our shared heredity, because it is the expression of a chemical and physical ordering of matter, makes each one of us a part of, and ought to make us feel at one with, the physical world from which we have evolved. But each one of us is also a literally unique expression of the world. This uniqueness is the inevitable result not only of a unique genetic background, but also of the specificity of the moulding experiences to which each of us has been subjected, both before and after birth. These are never identical for any two individuals, not even for so-called identical twins. What emerges, finally, from the process of development, is a unique person,

[1] 1930 (Revised Edition 1951), O.U.P.

and it is personality that makes it possible for us to engage in the highest human activity, namely to love.

According to Teilhard's law of complexity-consciousness the history of our world-in-evolution demonstrates beyond peradventure that along the time-axis there have developed both increasing degrees of complexity-in-organization and, *pari passu*, increasing levels of consciousness. By emphasizing (though not, to my mind, often enough) the essentially *groping* character of the evolutionary process, he is careful to control what would otherwise be an altogether too optimistic and naive interpretation of the world, many aspects of which must cause us to pause and say "but this is biological regress, not progress". That there is a tendency in evolution towards increasing complexity and increasing consciousness seems undeniable. But that the tendency is sometimes frustrated and sidetracked is equally undeniable. In LE MILIEU DIVIN Teilhard uses the word "diminishments" to describe certain facets of spiritual life. This penetrating expression is worthy of wider use, in other contexts. Study of the pathology as well as of the physiology of natural processes leads one to see "diminishments" in operation in a good many situations besides the adult human one.

It is important to appreciate that embryos suffer such diminishments to a very considerable degree. It has been calculated that in man, as is known more definitely to be the case in other mammalian species, the death-rate amongst embryos (and I speak here only of death from "natural causes") is at least thirty per cent. Most spontaneous abortions, or miscarriages, are probably the result of inborn errors in the makeup of the *conceptus*, many occurring before the fact of pregnancy was established or even seriously suspected. These genetic accidents form part and parcel of the mechanism of evolution, because they are the basis from which natural selection selects. There is increasing evidence also that a variety of environmental factors, again arising from natural causes, can harm the embryo in the womb. To be alive at all is to be at permanent risk. This incredible adventure, on which we all started some nine months before we were born, is fraught with perils at every stage. As the distinguished embryologist George Corner once observed, "Those of us who survive are truly the elect, chosen from a larger multitude[1]". Election carries responsibilities, and we do well to remember those whose candidature for survival was unsuccessful.

[1] G. W. Corner, OURSELVES UNBORN: AN EMBRYOLOGIST'S ESSAY ON MAN. 1944, Yale University Press.

Now if the human genetic complex, contained at fertilization within an egg the size of the smallest visible grain of sand, carries all the complex information necessary for the development of an individual to full maturity, is not the egg the most complicated cell of all? Is it right to think of subsequent development in terms of increasing complexity? And if not, what happens to the theory of complexity-consciousness? There is a paradox here, one that is inherent too in the Law we are considering, as expounded by Teilhard in terms of evolution. The ultimate end is somehow implied by, and contained within, the beginning. In fact the paradox is even more striking when one reflects that the potential is always wider in scope, and of greater significance, than the actual that is achieved. It seems to me unlikely that, at this early stage of exploration of the law of complexity-consciousness, we shall be in a position to resolve the paradox. I certainly am not. But a brief description, followed by an analogy, may help to direct the thoughts of better philosophers than I along profitable lines.

Embryologists speak of the fertilized ovum as a "totipotential cell". After its first cleavage-division the two daughter cells remain "totipotent": if separated from one another they are likely to give rise to two complete individuals. This is one of the ways in which identical twins arise. If, however, the cells remain united and continue to divide, there arises a small knot of cells we call a "morula" (literally a "mulberry"). All these cells are now called "pluripotent" because, although none of them is capable of giving rise to a whole individual, each is capable of forming any part of the individual-in-the-making it is called upon to make. With further multiplication of cells but continued union, some degree of specialization becomes inevitable. Teilhard's phrase, applicable here as in many other situations, is "union differentiates". Analysis of the ways in which initially identical cells in the embryo gradually specialize, become differentiated, and form the separate tissues and organs of which we are made, is one of the most intriguing aspects of professional embryological research. The complexities that reveal themselves are quite breathtaking in their scope and in their "audacity". Some of the first cells to specialize are those that will form no part of the baby after birth. These constitute the "extra-embryonic tissues and membranes". They are, in effect, special organs which meet the requirements of the developing embryo for oxygen and carbon-dioxide exchanges, for absorption of foodstuffs and for the elimination of the breakdown products of metabolism. Most remarkably, though, the embryo organizes its own environment by means of these extra-corporeal organs. One of their many functions is to elaborate, at a very early stage, complex hormones which act on the mother's body to prevent her having the menstrual period which would normally be expected some two weeks after fertilization, and which would, of course, be disastrous for the embryo. Moral theologians have committed themselves and the church to peculiar views at times about the status of these extra-embryonic structures, namely as to whether they are to be regarded as part of the individual or not. Although it is true they are discarded at birth, yet they are as much a part of the total organism *in utero* as are, say, the external gills of larval amphibians which are shed at metamorphosis. From the end of the first week in human embryology they constitute a literally vital part of this unique, developing organism. Subsequent differentiation and specialization of cells within the embryo itself show equally remarkable fitness and adaptation to the needs of the organism. Sometimes, of course, some necessary complexification falls short of perfection, and the result is congenital disease or death. As we have said, to be alive at all is to be at permanent risk, and the risks are greatest in the early stages. The surprising thing is not that some embryos fail to survive, but rather that so many contrive successfully to negotiate all the hazards through which they must pass.

Consciousness, as we know it in the human individual, would not be possible without this growth and differentiation of specialized cells, tissues and organs. Nor would it be possible without their acting in harmony and unison. When this two-way process is in full operation then the actualization of potential is maximized.

One can make an analogy at this point with groups of persons constituting a community. Any size of community will serve, from a small family-group upwards. Ultimately our aim must be really to experience the analogy in terms of the whole community of people that constitutes the human race. To illustrate my thesis, though, I will choose a community of intermediate size but of global significance. I sometimes make the suggestion, in my lectures to first-year medical students, that they should think of themselves as constituting, as a group, a sort of embryo at the morula-stage, each cell more or less alike, and all of them "pluripotent". During their formative years of medical study they will be subjected to a common discipline, but they will also have opportunity to explore the multiple pathways that are open to them in this attractive profession. As time goes on they find themselves, depending on individual interests and abilities, becoming separated out into specialist groups. But however specialized and narrow one becomes he still retains his membership of the profession, and maintains its common purpose, the relief of sickness and suffering. As with the cells of the human body, some of the most important work is carried out by those "cells" or "individuals" who specialize in being undifferentiated (if you will excuse the paradox), capable of fulfilling multiple roles, and of assuming a variety of special functions as required. The medical community is world-wide. Whether an individual member is a general surgeon or physician, or a specialist in some minute branch, whether he becomes a medical writer or a general practitioner, a teacher or laboratory scientist, he will always feel at home with fellow-members of the profession in any part of the world. Precisely out of the co-operation that follows from this unity-in-diversity, wholly new insights and advances in treatment are to be expected, and do of course arise, as we are all aware.

This is but one example, at the psycho-social stage of evolution, of the operation of Teilhard's law of complexity-consciousness. Given the potential, the dynamism, and the operation of natural selection in an evolutionary situation, something wholly new is bound to emerge. Each of us, through our personal embryological and postnatal history, represents another example of the operation of this important law. Complexity-consciousness is not only the means by which the world expresses itself in meaningful terms. It is also the means by which each of us acquires and expresses his own personality. It will, if we so choose, provide the key to the future of man and of his relationship to God.

# CHAPTER FOUR

## The Meaning of Life and History in Marx and Teilhard de Chardin: Teilhard's Contribution to the Dialogue between Christians and Marxists

by Roger Garaudy
Translated by Noël Lindsay

The affirmation that the world and history have a meaning is the focal point of the whole life's work of Father Teilhard de Chardin. It is both the starting point and the point of convergence of his experience as a scientist, of his faith as a Christian and of his needs as a man of action.

Any attempt to derive the affirmation that the world and history have a meaning purely from the needs of action, or purely from the faith of a Christian, or purely from the experience of the scientist, inevitably leads to a fatal dogmatism. Teilhard's genius lies in his seeking to surmount this compartmentation.

If the affirmation of meaning were purely a need of action, we should be faced with a variant of the pragmatism that professes to subordinate thought to action, in the name of the sole criterion of utility and efficacy. The meaning of the world and of history can then be either arbitrary or mystical, serving the ends of some specific action. The most bestial example of this attitude was given us by Hitler, proclaiming that the meaning of the world and of history was the triumph of the Aryan, and cultivating the racist myth in order to justify action designed to dominate the world and to enslave and destroy mankind.

With Father Teilhard, in contrast, the needs of action do not take the place of scientific knowledge, but, on the contrary, call it in aid and stimulate research.

In a very fine passage on "the fear of existence", Teilhard analyses the reasons for "mounting fear" in twentieth-century man. Ever since the first great scientific discoveries of the Renaissance, man might well feel himself lost in the immensity of the universe, might well experience a fatal vertigo. The traditional outlook of the Middle Ages had accustomed man to living in a closed world. And now this universe is *deprived of its centre* by astronomy, exploding the limits of Ptolemy's crystal spheres, which had thus far enclosed man and the earth in a reassuring chrysalis. Man and his planet are now no more than an infinitesimal and derisory point in the limitless infinity of the galaxies.

This universe is *deprived of its centre* by biology, which replaces the Bible stories of a mere six thousand years of dialogue between man and his God, by the savage epic of life, in which the two million years of human history and prehistory are no more than a brief episode in the full unfolding of life on our planet and the genesis of our minute planet in the cosmos.

This universe is *deprived of its centre* by psychology itself, since Freud has given us an image of man in which all sorts of fibres, drawn from the remote everywhere, compose our soul out of their monstrous nodes, ever ready to escape our control and become loosened.

How can man break away from the anguish of being thus thrown, like a wisp of straw, into this maelstrom of worlds, into an absurd universe, devoid of meaning, in which he is nothing?

There is a great temptation, and, for four centuries past, Christians have often yielded to it, to turn away from science and from a world where man is seized with such vertigo, and to oppose science with faith, this world with another world, to try vainly to preserve, in a century which has become storm-tossed, the changeless certainties of another age.

Father Teilhard dismisses this solution as ruinous. "The first source of modern unbelief," he writes, "is to be looked for in the illegitimate schism which, since the Renaissance, has gradually separated Christianity from what might be called the natural human religious stream."

Thus, faith in man and faith in God are opposed to each other with increasing violence.

Faith in man, which Teilhard calls the religion of the earth, is confidence in the power of reason and science, confidence in the future, in what the world, transformed by man, could become by our efforts, our labour and our struggles. "By faith in man," Teilhard wrote, "we mean the more or less active and passionate conviction that mankind, taken in its organic and organized totality, has a future before it; a future formed not only of the succession of years, but of higher states to be reached by way of conquest."

With this faith in man, stresses Teilhard, there reappeared, on the modern scale, the temptation of Prometheus and Faust, the temptation today of Marxism: "Why, in view of his own powers, should man seek a God outside himself? Man, entirely autonomous, sole master and solely responsible for his own destiny and the destiny of the world, is that not a much finer thing?"

In this encounter with Marxism, Teilhard, although he had no profound knowledge either of the teaching of Marx or of Marxists, sought to take its measure and grasp its significance.

His reflections on Marxism bear, in their hesitations and their contradictions, the mark both of this unfamiliarity and also of that attraction which finally enabled him to extract the essential.

At the outset he contents himself with an over-simplified opposition between the Christian spirit and what he calls "a Promethean or Faustian spirit of self-adoration, centred on the material organization of the earth", but he immediately adds, "this divergence is neither complete nor final, so long at least as (. . .) the Marxist, for example, has not eliminated from his materialism all upward drive towards the spirit".

Teilhard, though he never read Marx, confusedly recognizes that Marxism is not confined to a simple demand for greater material well-being. He even protests when he comes across such an interpretation. In a letter of 25 April 1954 on the subject of a study by Gusdorf on 'Christianity and Marxism', he writes: "Gusdorf considers almost exclusively the dispossessed in quest of well-being, and not sufficiently (often among these same poor wretches) the thirst for *fuller being*, the 'creation' of man on earth. Stronger and deeper than the sense of justice, I believe that what makes the contagious force of Marxism is its (illegitimate) monopolization of the sense of the Evolutive."

Teilhard rendered more and more justice to Marxism on realizing that the constant need for surpassment which animates it is inconsistent with the accusation of self-adoration, of smug self-satisfaction, with the accusation of limiting its human horizon to a simple technical organization of the earth. Teilhard writes: "Thirst for well-being in appearance, but in reality thirst for fuller being; mankind suddenly invaded by the sense of all it still has to do to arrive at the term of its power and its possibilities (. . .). Just like the collectivization which accompanies it, the ascent of human faith that we are witnessing is a life-bringing and therefore irresistible phenomenon." Teilhard considers this faith in man as a positive factor: it is the mainspring of the history from which we are emerging.

Siting his faith in God in relation to this faith in man, he adds: "Our faith in God sublimates in us a rising tide of human aspirations, and it is into this original sap that we must plunge back if we desire to communicate with the brothers whom it is our ambition to reunite." He concludes: "Are not the two extremes, the Marxist and the Christian, destined, in spite of their antagonistic concepts, because they are both animated by an equal faith in man, to find themselves together on the same summit?"

This theme was to remain a central theme of Teilhard's thought up to the end of his life, as when he wrote in a letter of June 1952: "As I like to say, the synthesis of the Christian God Above and the Marxist God Ahead is the only God whom we can henceforth adore in spirit and in truth."

It is therefore no accident that the first great fundamental dialogue between Marxists and Christians, which marked the starting point of so many other dialogues and set a new style for the human encounter of Christians and Marxists, was a debate between three Teilhardian Catholics and three Marxists, militant Communists, in Paris in 1960.

Contrary to a timid tradition, Teilhard does not seek to turn us away from the material world, from human effort, from scientific thought, by belittling them. It is, on the contrary, by magnifying them and exalting them that he integrates them in his synthesis. The synthesis of the Marxists can hear and understand him.

He first turns to science to find the foundation of his optimism and of a joyous and reasoned confidence in the human future.

The problem of the meaning of life and of history is then raised in a more general perspective, a cosmic perspective: "Has becoming any meaning? Is evolution directed? (. . .) We find ourselves faced with a problem of nature; to discover, if it exists, the meaning of evolution."

The overall answer which emerges from research is, according to Teilhard, this: "Let us look around us at the Universe in all its dimensions, psychic, spatial and temporal. In the heart of this interdependent and limitless immensity, in the inverse direction to a general tendency to running down and disintegration, we can detect a rising tide of complexification accompanied by consciousness."

Father Teilhard deploys this panorama of the upward movement of creation in THE PHENOMENON OF MAN. This outline of a synthesis of scientific knowledge, designed to discover the laws and the general meaning of becoming, is familiar to a Marxist, because he finds in it all the essential elements of Engels' Dialectic of Nature; the close Hegelian link between becoming and reciprocal action, the law of the transformation of quantity into quality, the master idea of Engels and Marx that evolution is no longer a hypothesis or a theory, but a fundamental category of all scientific thought, the passage, at the same time continuous and discontinuous, from inert matter to life, and from spontaneous life to reflective consciousness, an analogous description of "critical points", an identical formulation in Teilhard and in Engels, by which, in man, nature becomes conscious of itself and of its evolution, the striking parallel between the evocation by Teilhard of the birth of man and Engels' pages on the role of labour and the tool in the transformation of the ape into man.

Father Teilhard's greatness, therefore, lies not in the discovery of this "phenomenology", the principle of which was perceived by Hegel a century and a half ago, and explored by Engels a century ago, but in his effort to integrate this scientific conception of the world into a Christian faith which had never previously ceased to combat it.

The difficulty of the undertaking was great, not only because of the bitter opposition which it aroused in the Church, but also because of the temptation to jump to hasty conclusions and to make evolution say what only faith can say.

As his reflection becomes more and more profound, Father Teilhard elaborates a veritable theory of levels of consciousness in which he tries to yoke together science and faith, and to show that, far from being in opposition, each of them calls upon and completes the other, without thereby making either of them say what can be said only by the other.

Even in THE PHENOMENON OF MAN he already felt the need of these distinctions: "Is it not a universally accepted principle of Christian thought in its theological interpretation of reality that our minds should have different and successive planes of knowledge?"

Along these lines he was to give an increasingly critical definition of science, warning us against any dogmatic interpretation of his thought: "In spite of appearances," he writes, "the Weltanschauung which I propose in no way represents a fixed and closed system. There is no question here (it would be ridiculous!) of a deductive solution of the world à la Hegel, of a definitive frame of truth, but only of a series of axes of progression." How in effect could there be a final truth in a world which is not final?

Father Teilhard presents his conception of the meaning of life and history, his personal conception of evolution, as a hypothesis. In his ESQUISSE D'UN UNIVERS PERSONNEL he writes: "As a starting point for this attempt I choose the hypothesis, strongly suggested by the findings of biology, that consciousness has never ceased to grow through living creatures and that the personal reflecting form which it reaches in man is the most characteristic that we know."

The evolution that Father Teilhard needs, in order to link up with faith, is not indiscriminate; it must be an *ascendant* and *convergent* evolution; for the cosmos to be Christocentric, evolution must be anthropocentric.

Teilhard in no way seeks to disguise his postulates; he lists them in the very first lines of COMMENT JE CROIS.

No-one is therefore more opposed than he is to the positivist conceptions of science: "There are no pure facts," he wrote, "but every experience, however objective it may be, is inevitably wrapped up in a system of hypotheses the moment the scientist tries to formulate it."

Far from being "pre-Critique", as has sometimes been alleged against it, Teilhard's thought embodies the essence of Kant's teaching; without professing to take his stand in the midst of things and to say once and for all what they are, he never forgets that, whatever we say about things or about God, it is we who say it. On this point, moreover, he remains faithful, as Father de Lubac emphasizes, to the fundamental axiom of Thomist philosophy that by natural reason we cannot attain to God "in himself", but only to the relation which all things bear to him. "It seems established beyond discussion," writes Teilhard, "that things projected themselves for us 'as they are' on to a screen where we could watch them without being involved. (. . .) The objectivism of the physicists is tending to be reversed. Not only is the disturbing influence of the observer on the thing observed made manifest, in the sphere of material phenomena, at the lower frontier of sensible experience, but, taking the whole edifice of waves and particles constructed by our science, it is also becoming manifest that this imposing architecture contains at least as much of 'ourselves' as of the other."

We go out to meet things with our hypotheses and our models, and, in the last analysis, it is the practical criterion which determines their truth. "Physics," writes Teilhard, "knows no criterion for the truth of its developments except this success. (. . .) It is the success of the whole which will be decisive. If the edifice is not complete in itself, or if it contradicts part of experience, it is because the initial hypothesis is faulty and must be abandoned."

Father Teilhard does not hesitate to apply this criterion to religion itself. "In our eyes," he writes in his INTRODUCTION À LA VIE CHRÉTIENNE, "the decisive test of the truth of a religion cannot be anything except its ability to give a total meaning to the universe which is in the process of discovery around us. The 'true religion', if it exists, must, we think, be recognized, not by the lustre of some particular outstanding event, but by the sign that, under its influence and by its light, the world as a whole affords the maximum interest for our love of action."

This critical reflection of Teilhard puts us on our guard against the temptation to treat as an ontology what he himself puts forward as a phenomenology. The great synthesis which constitutes this phenomenology, this search for the "meaning" of life and history, remains a hypothesis which can be summed up as follows: the meaning of evolution is an ascent towards the personal. Man, who is the spearhead of this movement, gives a meaning to everything which precedes him. In contrast to the phenomenology of Husserl, for whom man gives a meaning to the world because he is free, in Teilhard's phenomenology, like that of Hegel, everything has a meaning *for* man because everything has a meaning *through* man; man apprehends the world as an organized whole, in movement to which his own appearance has given a meaning. This movement towards complexity-consciousness and towards personalization is not completed, with the result that the totality takes on its meaning from that which is still to come.

At this precise point faith interlocks with science. When Teilhard raises the problem of the relations between God and the world, it is natural that he should discover the point of contact in the God-Man, Jesus Christ. The relation between Christ and the world is at the centre of Father Teilhard's theology.

We must be careful here not to attribute to Teilhard the idea that science alone can solve this problem and define this relation unilaterally, as if science could absolve the believer from his faith: "Far be it from me, my friends, to think of deducing Christian dogmas solely from the inspection of the properties recognized by our reason in the structure of the world. Jesus Christ, by his most fundamental morale and his surest attributes, comes in most admirably to fill this void, marked by the expectation of all nature."

Even more forcibly, Teilhard writes in his LETTERS FROM A TRAVELLER: "The solution cannot be found except in a *faith* beyond all experience."

The centre of Teilhard's vision of the world is finally Christ; if we have noted at the outset that man *is* the meaning of the world, it must be added that this means man conscious of his mission to conduct evolution to its ultimate accomplishment of personalization and amorization, that is to say, what Teilhard calls "point Omega".

"The great event of my life," he wrote in 1953, "will have been the gradual identification, in the heaven of my soul, of two suns, one of these stars being the cosmic summit postulated by a generalized evolution of the convergent type, and the other being formed by the resurrected Jesus of the Christian faith."

It would be a false interpretation to deduce from this identification that, for Teilhard, Christ is nothing but point Omega, that the Parousia is merely the immanent culmination of evolution.

First, because Teilhard never hesitates to recall that the evolutionary ascent is not an inevitable movement. Men could reject the prospects of point Omega and we cannot rule out the frustration of the evolution begun millions of years ago; the technical possibility which exists today of wiping out all trace of life on earth by the destructive use of atomic and nuclear energy shows that this hypothesis is no mere imaginative speculation.

Next, because, if Teilhard considers that Christ is the meaning of history, he does not regard this certainty as the conclusion of a scientific demonstration. He in no way dissimulates the transition from what is scientifically plausible to what is necessary for action or in conformity with revelation. "I mean by *faith*," he writes, "every adherence by our intelligence to a perspective of the universe. (...) The keynote of the act of faith, in my opinion, is to perceive as possible and to accept as more probable, a conclusion which (. . .) goes beyond all the analytical premisses. To believe is to effect an intellectual synthesis."

At this level, an inversion of perspective takes place in the passage from simple scientific extrapolation to act of faith. "Seen from below, from our side of things, the vertex of the evolutive cone (point Omega) takes shape in the first place on the horizon as a simply immanent focus of convergence; Mankind totally reflected upon itself. But on examination, it proves that this focus, if it is to hold good, must have behind it, and deeper than itself, a transcendent divine nucleus."

E

There is therefore a twofold "wager" on the part of Teilhard, which comes in to break the serene continuity of immanent speculation: first, that of scientific extrapolation, which does not rule out the risk of the capsizing of evolution, for where man is, nothing is played out in advance; and, secondly, that of faith: "For a Christian," writes Teilhard, "the final biological success of man on earth is not only a probability, but a certainty, since Christ is risen. This certainty, however, derived as it is from a 'supernatural' act of faith, is of a supraphenomenal order. This means that, in a sense, it allows all the anxieties of man's estate to go on existing in the believer, at their own level."

Thus, Father Teilhard clearly emphasizes, as Claude Cuénot noted in one of their talks, that "faith is born only of faith" and that no scientific synthesis can absolve us, at every level, from the act of faith which is its foundation; the world has a meaning; this meaning is the spirit; the spirit moves towards unification and personalization; this movement is fully realized in Christ.

When Teilhard proclaims that Christ is the meaning of history, he does not mean by that merely that he is the meaning of sacred history. The Incarnation has its meaning not only in relation to the sin of man, which Christ is held to have come to redeem, and to lead mankind back on to the road towards its final goal, as though that Incarnation had not been foreseen in the original plan of creation, and became necessary only after the Fall and in order to remedy it. Father Wildiers has emphasized that, in this Thomist conception, "it is only in a guilty mankind that Christ has a function to fulfil, the function of Redeemer."

On the other hand, in the Franciscan or Scotist conception, Christ is the crown of the natural world, as of the supernatural order. Father Teilhard, carrying on this tradition, considers that Christ is the meaning, not only of sacred history, but of all human history and even of cosmic natural history.

Christ is therefore at the same time in a moral and juridical relation with men, and in an organic relation with the whole history of man, of life, and of the cosmos, of which he is the centre.

From this there flows, in Teilhard, a veritable theology of labour and of human effort, calling upon man to give himself up with all his might to his terrestrial task, and in no circumstances to allow himself to be diverted from it to attain eternal salvation.

Such is the primary significance of that INTRODUCTION À LA VIE

CHRÉTIENNE, in which Teilhard sketches the outlines of what might be a twentieth-century Christianity. "The Universe manifests itself to our generation," he writes, "as an organic whole on the march towards more liberty and ever more personality." He examines the different themes of Christian belief, in this resolutely evolutionary perspective, to try to establish that "Christianity is, by its very structure, the religion exactly made to measure for an Earth awakened to the sense of its organic unity and of its developments."

If it is true, in his phrase, that "God can act only evolutively" in the interior of the Whole, as its movement and its life, and not by arbitrary interventions, then the miracle no longer plays a dominant role in apologetics, and even changes its meaning: "The Christian miracle (that is to say, the manifestation of a divine personal influence in Christianity) is tending, in our eyes, to shift from the zone of 'prodigies of detail' to the zone of 'vital, general success of faith in Jesus'. Today (. . .) the capacity displayed by Christianity to direct, animate and plan human evolution (anthropogenesis) certainly makes us feel and recognize the hand of God in the world much more than any particular extraordinary happening."

Father Teilhard applies this principle to the uttermost, since he adds: "In a certain number of cases (the Virginity of Mary, the material Resurrection of Christ, the Ascension, and the like) we have the impression that the Gospel miracles do not so much represent concrete facts as an attempt to translate in a tangible way what is "irrepresentable" in such profound events as the immersion of the Word in the human phylum or the passage of Christ from his individual human state to his cosmic state as the centre of Evolution. Not only symbols, but the expression in images of the inexpressible."

Father Teilhard thus strikes a decisive blow at "integralism", that is to say, at that specifically Christian form of dogmatism (with all the inquisitorial forms which flow from it) which consists in confounding the Christian message with the cultural or institutional forms which Christianity may have happened to take at different periods in its history.

He thus joins the most vital streams of contemporary theology, from Father Laberthonnière to Father Rahner, and from Karl Barth to Bultmann, who have clearly established that what is "kerygmatic" must not be confused with what is historic; even if the Crucifixion is historic, what history can tell about it does not bring out its fundamental meaning. If the Resurrection were a problem of cellular physiology or reanimation, it would be hard to understand how it had managed to revolutionize the lives of millions of men for thousands of years.

A faith which depended on the experimental verification of this or that physical fact or the historical criticism of this or that text or evidence, would be in dire danger of being very quickly deprived of all foundation. Faith, in the most vital theology, appears more as the free response of man to the call of God. It is the moment of decision, lying between the past and the future. At every instant it affirms the possibility of a break with the vested order of nature and of history. It is in this way that it is conceived, in contrast with all the conceptions grafted on from Platonic or Aristotelian Hellenism, and in the prophetic spirit of Judaism, by Barth and Bultmann, and also by Father Rahner, when he defines Christianity as "the religion of the absolute future". It is this, also, which, for Father Teilhard, is fundamental in the Cross. In LE MILIEU DIVIN he sums it up in these words: "However marred by our faults, or however desperate in its circumstances our position may be, we can, at any moment, by a total re-ordering, completely correct the world that surrounds us, and resume our lives in a favourable sense."

The man who takes evolution in hand and transforms natural history is therefore a man of responsibility.

A Marxist is here both very near to Father Teilhard and very far from him.

Very far, in the first place. While Marxism, which is a conception of the world underlying a methodology of historic initiative, recognizes the decisive importance of the Christian moment of humanism, the moment of the opening up of man to a limitless future, in contrast with the Greek moment of humanism which makes man a part of a whole and of an order, of the City and of the Cosmos, and while it is conscious of the need to integrate this moment, it cannot accept it in the alienated form implied by the Christian act of faith; if for a Marxist, man is not merely the resultant of the natural or historical conditions which have engendered him, this break with the old order and this emergence of the new, this "transcendence" in a word, is not the attribute of a God, but the specific dimension of man.

It follows that, for a Marxist, the meaning of life and history is not a fact of *nature*, but a fact of *culture*. This meaning was not written by a

God on the first day of creation. It is the work of human history, from the appearance, with labour, with the first tool, with the first chipped flint, of the first human "project", anticipating the reality already fashioned and laying down the conscious goal of man as the law for the action exerted upon it, down to the extension of that human project to the prospects of Communism. Communism for Marx is the planetary (and perhaps cosmic) organization of needs, resources and hopes, by mankind made one and freely associating the work and thought of all men for a boundless transformation of nature, society and of themselves, the free development of the material and spiritual forces of man becoming an end in itself.

To us Marxists, that is the glorious meaning of life and history.

And thereby, finally, we also feel that we are very near to Father Teilhard; if we in no way share the act of faith in God which is his, we partake of his confidence in man.

For, if Father Teilhard has strongly emphasized that the Parousia is something other than the "point Omega", something other than the prolongation of the immanent evolution of the Earth, he is not one of those who consider that the Parousia has nothing to do with history; for him, on the contrary, the Parousia is not devoid of reference to the full blossoming of the world. In LE MILIEU DIVIN he magnificently proclaims: "(. . .) the progress of the universe, and in particular of the human universe, does not take place in competition with God, nor does it squander energies that we rightly owe to him. The greater man becomes, the more humanity becomes united, with consciousness of, and mastery of, its potentialities, the more beautiful creation will be, the more perfect adoration will become, and the more Christ will find, for mystical extensions, a body worthy of resurrection."

Father Teilhard's work constitutes a decisive ground for meeting and dialogue between Christians and Marxists, by stressing that the concrete development of humanity and of its institutions, science, the state, labour, culture, art, civilizations, have a decisive significance in the Christian perspective.

For us Marxists, religion is an opium whenever it teaches that in order to reach God you must turn your back on the world, for that is the sovereign alibi of all the forces of historical regression.

Father Teilhard has opened up for our age the prospect of another form of Christian spirituality which bids the faithful not to renounce the world, but, on the contrary, to bend all his energy towards transforming the world into a more human world, that is to say a world at once more conscious, more unified and more personal.

To have formulated the problem in this way constitutes a capital contribution to the dialogue between the living, even if Father Teilhard hardly gives us any concrete means of solving it, owing to the fact that he regards social progress as merely one of the aspects of biological progress. This failure to recognize the specific nature of the level of the social threw him off his course among the concrete forms of political and social organization, as witnessed, for example, by some of his judgments in 1935 on the historical significance of Fascism, in which he thought he could discern a positive will, or again, in 1952 on Communism, when he wrote: "The only way to conquer Communism is to present Christ as he should be; not opium (or a derivative) but the essential driving force of a Hominization which can only be energetically consummated in a world open at the summit and 'amorized'."

The problem here is badly put, since the essential is omitted, namely the concrete problems of economic, political and social organization. If they are given their full place, taking account of the political and social role played historically by the Church in the conservation of the established disorder, and of the concrete historical requirement represented by Marxism, Teilhard's formula can then be rephrased: "The only way to overtake Communism is to put an end to the internal contradictions of the social system which engendered it," but then Communism will not be conquered, it will be realized. Teilhard's marvellous ambition "to present Christ as he should be; not opium (or a derivative) but the essential driving force of a Hominization which can only be energetically consummated in a world open at the summit and 'amorized' " will also be realized. Only the union of these two great forces can raise up the world, without victors or vanquished, in a synthesis which alone can give their highest meaning to the life of men and to the world.

Father Teilhard summoned us to this when he called for a common front of those who believed in the future and who held themselves responsible for bringing about its progress, and when he added, in a letter from abroad: "There is only one way of discovery, it is to construct the future."

Teilhard's thought leads to a philosophy of action: "The problem of knowledge," he wrote, "tends to be coordinated with, or better, to be subordinated to, the problem of action." Claude Cuénot was right in emphasizing this profound analogy when he wrote: "Complete spirituality is for Father Teilhard what true philosophy is for Karl Marx, a praxis." Labour is prayer.

For Teilhard, as for Marx, it is one and the same thing to think that life has a meaning and to hold oneself responsible for its fulfilment, it is one and the same thing to *receive* that meaning through knowledge and to *give* it through action, to live it as knowledge and as militant responsibility.

That is the deep meaning of our dialogue: between two confronting dogmatisms, equally assured of possessing a complete and finite verity about the meaning of life and of the world, no dialogue is possible, but only a crusade between two fanaticisms. And a crusade in the present state of the techniques of destruction means the annihilation of mankind; the human epic, begun two million years ago, would thus, in coming to an end, lose all its significance. Dialogue, in our days, is an essential condition if life and the world are to have a meaning.

At the same time this dialogue has become particularly difficult because of the development of techniques and the technocratic organization of the division of labour to which that development leads. Millions of human existences are identified with the function imposed upon them and which assigns a meaning to their life "from outside", that is to say, deprives it of human significance. Dialogue, in our days, is one of the essential conditions for overcoming the mutilations and unilateralism of the division of labour.

It is an infantile reaction and an impotent reaction to try to compensate this solitude and this mutilation by claiming the rights of a self-enclosed subjectivity, of the existentialism which attributes to the abstract liberty of the individual and solitary consciousness the illusory power of giving a meaning to things and to life.

The merit of Teilhard's phenomenology, in contrast to the fashionable solipsist phenomenologies and in line with Hegel and Marx, is that it is conscious of the indissoluble links between my existence and that of the universe.

The problem of the meaning of my personal life cannot be divorced from that of the meaning of history and the meaning of the cosmos.

The problem is not purely theoretical, it is practical, too: without a historical programme we cannot discover the meaning of our own life.

With the entry of man into cosmic space, and with the new responsibilities which mankind thus assumes by taking part in the transformation no longer of his own planet alone, but of the universe, we shall perhaps soon have to stop speaking of a planetary historical programme and speak of a cosmic programme in order to give our lives their full meaning.

The solutions which we can put forward to this immense problem of the meaning of life and of the world may no doubt differ. We Marxists are materialists, that is to say that we try to answer the questions of man without bringing in the postulates of an "other world". In the words of our poet Aragon, *"The answer to the question, Who am I? is: I am of this world."*

Christians have made another choice. Our dialogue will be fruitful if the answers which each of us gives do not evade the real questions put by the other. For answers are only given a meaning by the questions put, and the fatal vertigo of dogmatism is to claim to give answers where no questions are asked.

Teilhard knew how to listen to the questions of the world before trying to give the answers of tradition alone.

It is up to us Marxists to listen to the questions of Teilhard, and, beyond him, of Christianity, by trying much more to understand what is fundamental in them than to dwell on the forms which shock us. Whatever objections the scientist, the philosopher or the theologian may raise against Teilhard, the important thing is the breach which he has opened in the ancient dogmatism of his Church, thus helping it to open up to the world, in a spirit to which the Second Vatican Council was not an entire stranger, and making possible the great dialogue of the twentieth century between all those who love man and his future.

Beyond all the subaltern polemics we should stand fast by this message, following the marvellous teaching of the Buddhist proverb, "When a finger points to the moon, the fool looks at the finger."

# CHAPTER FIVE

## *Marxism, Evolution and The Person of Christ*

by Anthony O. Dyson

In an article contributed to the French literary periodical EUROPE,[1] Professor Roger Garaudy quoted the following dictum of Teilhard de Chardin. "As I like to put it, the synthesis between the (Christian) God 'above' and the (Marxist) God 'in front': here is the only God whom we can henceforth adore in spirit and in truth."[2]

I will now cite Garaudy's comments on this statement and use the two as a starting-point for a modest theological contribution to Marxist-Christian dialogue along the lines suggested by my title.

"However bold and comprehensive this formula may be for a Christian, a Marxist can accept it neither in form nor content, for his movement 'forward' is not inspired by religious faith, and he repudiates the God 'above'. Precisely at this point there is, between Christians and Marxists, an irreducible and fundamental opposition. We Marxists do not think that there is an *end* to the progress of man. Communism is not for us the end of history, but the end of pre-history and the beginning of a characteristically human history stretching into the infinite distance. Even less do we think that this end could be 'beyond'. As atheists, nothing is promised to us and nothing awaits us. Thus encounter cannot occur in this area."[3]

It might seem unlikely that a fruitful discussion can be initiated on the basis of so uncompromising a statement. There would be no such difficulty if instead I had selected one of Garaudy's many thoughtful and stimulating remarks about the elaboration of a Marxist humanism, and plunged without more ado to discuss the relation of such a humanism to Christianity. For, *a priori*, Christian faith can dialogue with any kind of humanism, since it is itself a humanism, though claims to be

---

[1] *Le père Teilhard, le Concile et les Marxistes*, EUROPE, March-April 1965, p. 206.
[2] In a letter dated 2 April 1952. This theme is developed in THE FUTURE OF MAN, London, 1964, p. 260 ff.
[3] Garaudy, *op. cit.*, p. 207.

more besides. But I cannot help feeling that to by-pass the question of God at this stage, to regard it from the beginning as an impasse in the dialogue, is a serious procedural mistake. It can only emaciate the discussion between Christians and Marxists, depriving it of depth and of a certain honesty.

Thus I have consciously chosen the foregoing quotation from Garaudy as indicating an axial point of dispute between Christians and Marxists. Some would regard this as a somewhat sterile subject for debate, the "blind alley of the Marxist critique of religion and the Christian penchant for transcendence".[1] This is true only in one sense, namely that it is no longer possible or profitable to traffic with the theism/atheism polarity as it was framed in Marx's day. Marx's positive assertions, as well as his critique of religion, were historically conditioned by the politico-economic situation of his day, as well as by the reaction against Hegel. Since then, both Marxism and Christianity have undergone much evolution and many inner transformations, so that in an important respect the classical formulation of Marxist atheism versus Christian theism is only of antiquarian interest. Moreover if we give any credence to Teilhard's understanding of psycho-social evolution, then we may hope that these evolutions and transformations have a positive and forward-looking character. We shall expect that in certain essential matters of truth Marxism and Christianity have evolved in some small measure towards each other, have converged rather than diverged. At least such a hypothesis is worth testing. For these reasons I claim that it is legitimate and useful to pose the question of God anew—especially to the current of thought represented by Professor Garaudy—to pose it positively in terms of what Christian theology is now saying, and negatively in relation to contemporary Marxist criticism.

It goes without saying that I have broached an intricate and even delicate subject about which much has been and continues to be written. In the present limited context I must simply submit some stray reflections. I will briefly sketch something of Garaudy's criticism of the traditional Christian notion of God. I shall go on to accept most of the force of that criticism. And finally I shall say something about a more responsible way for Christians to discourse about God, which is at one and the same time more faithful to the Biblical witness, more consonant with the nature of the world as we know it, and also goes some way

[1] I. Hermann, *Total Humanism: Utopian Pointers between Coexistence and Pluralism*, CONCILIUM, June 1966, p. 76.

to meeting the proper Marxist objections. In this last section I shall draw on Teilhard's thought, in particular on the way he "coheres" the person of Christ and evolution.

Garaudy, in the article already quoted and in his remarkable little book FROM ANATHEMA TO DIALOGUE,[1] seems to make three main objections to the Christian notion of God, (i) that he is "above", i.e. outside and beyond human history, (ii) that he is externally poised to guillotine the march of human history at some arbitrary but definite point in the future, (iii) and because of the first two points, that this notion of God's transcendence is an alienating factor for man in that it purports to solve his intellectual problems from outside, and that it puts a brake on the Promethean soaring of the human adventure by being an absolute rival to human independence.

This raises the question whether Garaudy's rejection in fact constitutes a rejection of theism in any final sense of the word, or whether he is rejecting one particular conceptual framework in which the idea of God has been presented. I shall contend that the latter is the case. I shall suggest that Garaudy's objections (which he presents with refinement where I have summarized them crudely) repudiate the main outlines of what may be called *classical theism*.

At the theological level the question is now widely posed as to whether the God of classical theism is not so far removed from God proclaimed in Old and New Testaments as to bear little resemblance to him. The God of classical theism, a timeless, a-social and absolute being, Pascal's "God of the philosophers", the God arrived at by Aquinas' five ways and by Descartes' mind-matter bifurcation, the God demolished with such vigour by Kant and Hume, seems to be the invention of metaphysicians, framed in part through a fusion of Platonic and Aristotelian strands, and by analogy with the "laboratory" methods of an emerging natural science. The gradual erosion of this notion of God is no new phenomenon and is not confined to Marxist analyses. Over the last 150 years it has been subjected to assaults from all sides. In the natural sciences it is an extraneous, intervening God who has been unseated. As Charles Kingsley put it, "Now they have got rid of an interfering God—a master-magician as I call it—they have to choose between the absolute empire of accident and a living, immanent, ever-working God".[2] In philosophy it is an Absolute Being, absolute by

[1] London, 1967, See esp. p. 78 ff.
[2] Quoted in L. C. Birch, NATURE AND GOD, London, 1965, p. 52.

analogy with our relative and contingent being, who has been deposed. Freudian psychology too has dissolved this notion of God by other means. Modern literature is studded with versions of this rejection, such as, to quote random examples, Rilke[1], Samuel Beckett and the Theatre of the Absurd. Existentialism must also be understood in part as a protest against the God of classical theism. Martin Heidegger's recourse to the Pre-Socratic philosophers and to the poetry of Hölderlin in search of a pre-logical mode of thought is not obscurantism but an attempt to escape from the objectifying, reifying tendencies of the philosophical tradition which has shaped Western culture and religion.

I have laboured this point at some length since for our present dialogue it is to my mind essential to recognize that what often seems *prima facie* to be a repudiation of theism as such, is more likely to be a repudiation of one form of theism, namely what I have called "classical theism". Conversely this means that we must be on our guard against an overly loose assignation of the word "atheism". We must be considerate enough to define what sort of theism is not being believed. And in this respect I would side with Schubert Ogden when he writes, "What distinguishes Western humanity today is not a greater degree of existential distrust of God but an ever more widespread theoretical dissent from the assertions of classical theism."[2]

It is precisely along these lines that Bishop Robinson's Frankfurt lecture 'Can a truly contemporary Person *not* be an Atheist?' must be understood. In this lecture he largely accepts the atheist critique that God is intellectually superfluous, emotionally dispensable and morally intolerable, i.e. God "as 'God' has been traditionally understood".[3]

Two features of this classical theism are particularly relevant to

---

[1] "And therefore all the forms of the here and now are not merely to be used in a time-limited way, but, so far as we can, instated within those superior significances in which we share. *But not in the Christian sense* (from which I more and more passionately withdraw), but, in a purely terrestrial, deeply terrestrial, blissfully terrestrial consciousness, to instate what is *here* seen and touched within the wider, within the widest orbit—that is what is required. Not within a Beyond, whose shadow darkens the earth, but within a whole, within *the whole*." R. M. Rilke in a letter to his Polish translator quoted in SONNETS TO ORPHEUS, ed. Leishman, London, 1949, p. 18.
[2] S. M. Ogden, *The Christian Proclamation of God to Men of the So-called 'Atheistic Age'*, CONCILIUM, June 1966, p.48.
[3] THE NEW REFORMATION, London, 1965, p. 106 f.

my present argument. 1. The whole natural and historical process which we call the cosmos is unrelated to this God's being. Indeed the traditional doctrine of redemption in the West is concerned with the rescue of man *from* the process. What is required is a form of world-denying goodness which will ensure one's safe deliverance from this vale of tears into heaven.[1] In the words of the Anglican burial service, death delivers us out of the miseries of this sinful world. Since the redemption of man has already been achieved potentially by the work of Christ, it only remains for God to consummate Christ's act by an arbitrary fiat which will bring the world to an end. 2. Negatively the effect of this idea of salvation is to pronounce the sentence of meaninglessness upon human effort, upon labours to create a better world. The future is closed and determined, and nothing that man does can materially affect the destiny of the cosmos. In other words, a static view of God, Christ and redemption is imposed upon a statically conceived world so that man is treated as an unhistorical being.

Now clearly in the space of one paragraph I have given only a caricature of the main sores on the visage of traditional theism. But I would be prepared to defend my criticism in fuller detail, and would insist that this world-view has penetrated deeply into the Christian introspective conscience of the West, as is illustrated in hymnody, liturgy, preaching and popular apologetic. We can therefore accept the Marxist criticism of classical theism as largely justified. On the other hand there is no need to suffer a bad conscience from this. For this particular framework for theism, like all formulations of doctrine, is a historically conditioned and relative phenomenon whose empirical genesis it is perfectly possible to trace, if we have the time, skill and energy, with the appropriate scholarly tools. It has moreover served its purpose in the past, for example by ridding the world, in principle at least, of fate and chance, and so providing the ordered cosmos in which the scientific method could grow. But we must now recognize that the objections to the God of classical theism are so grave that we must think again.

For Christian theology the whole picture has been changed by two complementary factors. 1. The invalidation of Biblical fundamentalism by the historical-critical movement of the nineteenth and twentieth

---

[1] Cf. Teilhard's CHRISTOLOGIE ET ÉVOLUTION (unpublished). "Until now the Christian was brought up under the impression that, to attain God, one had to let everything go." p. 10.

centuries. The effect of this has been to rob the events of the Biblical narrative of an extrinsic dogmatic status guaranteed by a theory of inspiration, and to return them to the single stream of human history in which they occurred and belong. Thus it is now no longer defensible to accommodate an inappropriate philosophy or cosmology to the Biblical narrative by the forced use of proof texts, and thus give that philosophy or cosmology canonical status. 2. The historical revolution, which began in the late eighteenth century with the work of the Göttingen historians, and developed under the impact of the Romantic Movement, and the scientific revolution of the nineteenth century (especially Darwinism) have rendered the static world-view as inappropriate for theology as atomism is for modern physics. Consequently theology finds itself compelled to submit to a new Copernican revolution. Teilhard, in the very important but unpublished essay CHRISTOLOGIE ET ÉVOLUTION, from which I quoted earlier, wrote that the recent and still incomplete transformation which has caused the universe to be seen not as a static reality but as an evolutionary reality, bears all the marks of a profound and definitive development.[1]

The repercussions of Teilhard's evolutionary hypothesis upon theology are formidable.

"Let us look honestly at the world as it presents itself today to the light of our reason. Not a world 4,000 years old, encircled by its 8 or 9 spheres, in terms of which the theology of our text-books was written, but the universe which we now see emerging organically from an unlimited time and space."[2]

His view of cosmogenesis means that theology has to come to terms with the fact of a real past and a real future. It means that all theology is located in a changing, becoming world, to which the language of classical theism is irrelevant. Thus Teilhard writes, "My profound conviction is that we have precisely arrived at this delicate point of necessary readjustment."[3]

Now if the rest of this paper is to be understood in logical succession to what I have said so far, it is essential to grasp at what point Teilhard begins his work of theological readjustment. He starts, not

[1] p. 2.
[2] Ibid.
[3] Op. cit., p. 1.

with the doctrine of God, but with the person of Christ. This is a crucial feature of Teilhard's methodology and holds out many important implications which I shall mention later. It has been rightly said that to "amputate [his oeuvre] of its Christological dimension would be to mutilate it irrevocably". "Christ is the key-stone of his vision."[1]

Now at first sight it might seem as if Teilhard is simply replacing one alienating, transcendent factor (the God of classical theism) by another (the Christ of the traditional creeds). But this is not the case. Applying the traditional notion of the Incarnation to an evolutionary cosmos where "the existence of the least monad is found to be linked and synchronized to the total evolution of things",[2] it follows that Christ's assumption of "flesh" unites him immanently to the whole cosmic order at every level, and to past, present and future. And since for Teilhard "God does not present himself to finite beings as an immediately graspable entity except in Christ", it follows too that the only way we can properly talk about God at all is in terms of Christ as immanent and operative within the known cosmos.[3] This is borne out when we examine the titles which Teilhard gives to Christ. The historical Christ, a historical phenomenon within the cosmic order. The evolutive Christ, animating the total evolution of the cosmos from within. The humanizing Christ, supporting and provoking the progressive humanization of the cosmos. The universal Christ, the immanent centre of the cosmos. The Omega Christ, animating the cosmos to a point of maturity where he will be instrumental to its achieving its ultimate destiny, which is a mystery we know nothing about.

"It is time, under the pressure of the facts, to return to a physical, more organic form of Christology. A Christ who is not only the master of the world because he has been declared such, but because he animates everything from top to bottom, a Christ who does not only dominate the history of heaven and earth because these have been given to him,

---

[1] A. Ligneul, *Perspective Christocentrique de Teilhard*, REVUE INTERNATIONALE PIERRE TEILHARD DE CHARDIN, March 1965, p. 5.
[2] CHRISTOLOGIE ET ÉVOLUTION, p. 8.
[3] C. Cuénot, LEXIQUE TEILHARD DE CHARDIN, Paris, 1963, article *Dieu*. Cf. "By his Incarnation (Christ) inserted himself not only into Humanity, but into the Universe which bears Humanity—not only by way of being an associated element, but with the dignity and function of a directing principle, of a Centre to which all love and affinity converge." ÉCRITS DU TEMPS DE LA GUERRE, Paris, 1965, p. 47.

but because his gestation, birth and gradual consummation represent the only definitive reality in which the evolution of the world can be honestly expressed."[1]

Why however are the functions of Christ located immanently within the cosmos? Teilhard's answer to this question brings me towards the final stage of my argument. The answer is, in very bare terms, that the evolution and final destiny of the cosmos depend upon human activity. He claims that in the nature of things (literally!) these goals are not achieved by a *deus ex machina* but by human effort. And Christ is found, to faith, immanent within the cosmos as the focus and energy of that effort but not as a substitute for it. There are many theological texts in Teilhard which express this. To quote only two, "Christ, as we know, fulfils Himself gradually through the ages in the sum of our individual endeavours."[2] "With each one of our *works*, we labour—in individual separation, but no less really—to build the Pleroma; that is to say, we bring to Christ a little fulfilment."[3]

For our present discussion it must be noted above all how in this view there is a long, open future. Only at the level of a personal, existential risk can a Christian hold the outcome to be assured. Such an assurance will be of a similar order to Lady Julian of Norwich's "all shall be well, . . . all manner of things shall be well". We fall again into the error of classical theism if we invoke the transcendence of God to guarantee in advance a successful outcome to evolution. Teilhard's empirical placing of human effort *vis-à-vis* a genuine future precludes such a step. Jürgen Moltmann has written, and it is an idea more fully developed in his THEOLOGIE DER HOFFNUNG, "Man obeys the will of God when he leaves the 'safe fortress' of his social shell and, on the horizon of the future allowed by God, he devotes himself to the alteration of the world and thus enters into history itself."[4]

Thus Moltmann wants to say, in theological language, that God's divinity will only be declared with the coming of his Kingdom, which is "not yet". It is therefore completely compatible with Christian faith to

---

[1] CHRISTOLOGIE ET ÉVOLUTION, p. 9.
[2] THE FUTURE OF MAN, p. 22.
[3] LE MILIEU DIVIN, London, 1964 (pb), p. 62.
[4] J. Moltmann, *Hope without Faith: An Eschatological Humanism without God*, CONCILIUM, June 1966, p. 19. Cf. also Karl Rahner's notion of God as "absolute future" (*absolute Zukunft*).

say that *knowledge about* God as he is in himself also belongs to the "not yet". Our cognitive faculties as human beings relate only to the empirical order and are therefore in principle incapable of encompassing transcendence as such. Only through an insistence—such as Teilhard's —on the total embodiedness of Christ in the empirical order, does man have any alternative to silence on the subject of God. Thus the following statement of Teilhard is infinitely more important than he makes it appear in its context. "If we may slightly alter a hallowed expression, we could say that the great mystery of Christianity is not exactly the appearance, but the transparence, of God in the universe."[1] This, as I understand it, is not a slight alteration but a fundamental shift in outlook. To apply the word "appearance" to God is to invite the discredit which belongs to all traditional transcendence-language. The word "transparence" is however perfectly congruous with the immanental perspective Teilhard provides in his concept of Christogenesis.

It may be that at this point I am pressing Teilhard's thought beyond his own intentions. I am unsure whether he realized just how far his cohering of Christ and evolution implies a far-reaching restatement of transcendence-language. I will illustrate my point with a quotation from Christopher Mooney's excellent study TEILHARD DE CHARDIN AND THE MYSTERY OF CHRIST. In his concluding critical appraisal of the "risks" in Teilhard's thought, Mooney writes,

"Neither the Christian nor the Church can conceive their mission chiefly in terms of fostering evolution, even when this is seen to be growth in spirit and personal fulfilment in the realm of knowledge and love. In the life of the individual Christian as well as in the life of the Church as a whole there is an immediate and transcendent relationship to the Person of Christ which is independent of all human progress and which cannot be reduced to any mere human energy."[2]

If we take these words at their face value, then far from just describing a "risk" in Teilhard's thought, they in fact seem to me to undermine the essential substance of his vision. In Teilhard's cohering of Christogenesis and cosmogenesis, in his concept of Christification, it is *precisely* the role of the Christian and the Church to foster evolution as a growth in spirit and personal fulfilment in the realm of knowledge and love.

[1] LE MILIEU DIVIN, p. 131.
[2] London, 1966, pp. 208 f.

F

For that evolution subsumes the whole purpose of creation, incarnation and redemption. Moreover I am inclined to view Mooney's stand for the "immediate and transcendent relationship to the Person of Christ" as an expression of that docetist tendency in Christology which has so often been *de facto* the doctrine of the Church when *de jure* it has been recognized as heresy. It seems to me that Teilhard's thoroughgoing interpretation of the Incarnation as rooting Christ physically and organically to the whole process of evolution implies that our relation to Christ is always mediate, not immediate, and is realized not in reflection, but (consciously or unconsciously) in human *deeds* (deeds of love, suffering, political action, etc.).[1]

There is no objection to using "transcendental" language as long as we realize that on this view it performs as "convictional" language (Zuurdeeg), as the language of existential understanding (Ogden). It is not language which gives us privileged information about the nature and purposes of God as a super-entity existing alongside and analogous with lesser, relative human entities, but rather the language, articulated around the person and function of Christ, which expresses "the conviction that comes from being grasped by the importance of some things over others".[2] Such language can therefore only be confirmed in experience and deeds. Thus Christians and Marxists live in one world and have the same information at their disposal.

Along these lines, I suggest, may be forged the beginnings of a methodological *rapprochement* between Christians and Marxists, to which the Marxist charge of alienation is no longer applicable.

In summary then, Teilhard's formulation of the function of Christ (i) respects the dignity of this world and human *joie de vivre*, (ii) respects

---

[1] This is in my opinion the relevance of Teilhard's energetics to his Christology. See volume VI, esp. pp. 143 ff., of the French edition of Teilhard's works. See also the interesting essay by Jacques and Anne-Marie Debelmas *Le Travail humain et sa Finalité*, in LA PAROLE ATTENDUE, Cahiers 4, Paris, 1963. Thus the language of transcendence is exploratory rather than explanatory since it emerges from the risk of intellectual synthesis. I have not attempted in this paper to work out any of the positive implications of Teilhard's thought for a Christian doctrine of God. I have simply pointed out that the *under*development of this doctrine in traditional theism has had disastrous consequences, but that Teilhard has indicated some essential lines along which proper development may take place. In this respect see the final chaper of Leslie Dewart, THE FUTURE OF BELIEF, London, 1967.
[2] Birch, *op cit.*, p. 117.

the autonomy of science, the impulse of research and all other forms of human effort which seek directly or indirectly to socialize and unify man, (iii) respects the existence of a genuine future which an as yet incomplete evolution logically requires. I believe that if these insights are brought to the Marxist-Christian dialogue, they can not only give added extent and depth to the search for a common humanist credo, can not only awaken Christians to the seriousness for themselves of the political and economic theses at the centre of Marxism, but can also stimulate Marxism, within a developing humanism, to reconsider the relation of the Biblical witness to God and Christ to its own thought and action. I am not suggesting that all this is round the corner, but I do claim that Teilhard has restored to Christian thinking the perspectives which can make it possible.

At the end of Teilhard's essay 'We must save Mankind', the French editor added this footnote:

"Father Teilhard de Chardin did not exclude from Christianity anyone who expressly or implicitly believes in Love. He knew that the hour is not the same for every man to realize that this Essential Love, cause and purpose of the Universe, is to be found at the very heart of the Universe."[1]

This is an accurate exegesis of Teilhard and I will add a comment to it in order to bring my remarks to a close.

It is an accurate exegesis of Teilhard because, as we have seen, he held Christ to be the universal, immanent centre of the cosmos in evolution, the source of energy and love, the focus of human effort. It follows that the autonomy of non-Christian world-views is to be radically respected where in some broken but recognizable sense love is found to be operative. (Such love, it must be admitted, seems often equally broken as practised by those people who understand it as deriving explicitly from Christ.) So the passionate concern of Marxists to build the city of man in freedom from oppression, their faith in the future of man, are (where they obtain) values which the Christian must recognize as concrete, but incognito and veiled, manifestations of the same love which he affirms is focussed in Christ. Love is not Christian because Christians do it, but because, recognized or unrecognized as such, it has its focus in the evolutive and humanizing Christ. That

[1] CONSTRUIRE LA TERRE, Cahiers 1, Éditions du Seuil, Paris, 1958, p. 12.

Marxism in its brief history has often led to oppression and cruelty does not count against what I have said. That is unless the inhumanity of Christian man to man, which has scarred the 2000 years of Christian history, is to be allowed to count against our own deepest values and convictions.

It was certainly Teilhard's understanding that political systems must, on the basis of complexity-consciousness, be allowed to develop to their fullest maturity, and that this process is, in the long run, one of convergence and centration. But there is every sign that what Teilhard called planetization is already well advanced, and that cross-fertilization and union between the positive threads of its different systems are urgently required. In Christianity at present, and I suspect in Marxism too, there is a shaking of the foundations. For Anglicans it may be symbolized by HONEST TO GOD, for Roman Catholics by the Second Vatican Council. Some see this upheaval as a threat to security and a call to revisit the past. In Teilhard's perspective the contemporary crisis must be positively interpreted as a threshold which man must cross if he is to reach the next stage of evolution, in the confidence that, to quote Charles Hartshorne, "becoming is no longer the enemy of permanence but its everlasting foundation". I would hold that the present stirrings of Marxist-Christian dialogue—and I am realist enough to be aware how puny they are—are a sign of this threshold and invite us to grasp the opportunity boldly and prosecute it vigorously.

The main condition which Teilhard prescribed for evolution to continue at the level of man was "an *irreversible* rise towards the *personal*".[1] Failing this "everything at the level of Man will cease to move".[2] He went on, "This surely means that the faith which finally triumphs must be the one which shows itself to be more capable than any other of inspiring man to action."[3] Marxism and Christianity are both, in their founding charters, revolutionary movements committed to action. In both there are at this moment minorities seeking to renew and rediscover the personalist element which must inform that action if it is not to be destructive. I have simply tried to open up one or two avenues of theoretical *rapprochement* in the conviction that to pursue entirely separate ways is for Marxism and Christianity a mutual impoverishment and an evolutionary blind-alley. If our common task

[1] THE FUTURE OF MAN, p. 207.
[2] *Ibid.*
[3] *Op. cit.*, p. 208.

is, in Teilhard's words, to personalize, to the extent of making it lovable, the time-space totality of Evolution, then such going-it-alone is also an act of irresponsibility. For a task of such dimensions involves all the resources of all men. I am sure there is a role in England for such dialogue between Marxists and Christians as we find now in France and Germany,[1] as long as we remind ourselves that dialogue is not enough, that we are to go on to work out the concrete implications of our co-reflection, seek to execute them and so build the earth (*construire la terre*).

---

[1] Though it must be conducted with our different English situation in mind.

# CHAPTER SIX

## The Christology of Pierre Teilhard de Chardin

by Francis G. Elliott

Translated by Noël Lindsay

1. The importance of the vision of the world proposed by Teilhard de Chardin and its attraction for our contemporaries arise not only because he has thrown light on the significance and universal character of evolution, but also because he has shown that evolution alone enables us to understand Man's place in the Universe, where he has hitherto felt overwhelmed and lost. It fell to the author of THE PHENOMENON OF MAN to discover in evolution the key concept of the meaning of being. Through this concept a dynamic vision of the world is built up in his work, through which man rediscovers himself participating with others in the movement of general unification which uplifts the Universe towards its ultimate Centre.

Teilhard explains, at the end of a report on his scientific activities, that he conceived this vision of the World when, by a slow coming together "which took place in his mind between the kindred concepts of the genetic structure of fauna and the genetic structure of the continents, there gradually emerged a third concept, that of the genetic structure of Mankind, considered as a biological unit of planetary scale" (Cahier, No. 5, p. 166). The text might be completed by adding: "The genetic structure of Mankind, considered as a biological unit of planetary scale and centred on Christ." These last words were obviously omitted from a report addressed to the Collège de France with a view to his nomination to the Chair of Palaeontology, but they nevertheless exactly complete, as we know from his other writings, his thought on Christ, or, as the theologians say, his "Christology". This is not a very happy term; the word is clumsy and somewhat pedantic and has a very doctrinal ring, whereas we must never forget—and Teilhard certainly never forgot—that we are speaking not of a thing, but of a person and of a transcendent person at that. Subject to this caveat the Christology of Teilhard de Chardin can be defined as follows: "Christ the foundation of Cosmogenesis" or again, "Christ yesterday, today and to all eternity, the source, condition and end of the evolution of the Universe." This is, in effect, a paraphrase of St. Paul's words to the Colossians: "All things were created by him, and for him, and he is before all things, and by him all things consist."

2. The Christology we have to deal with here will seem somewhat daring in the light of our rather fixed ideas of faith, and does not fit easily into static or rationalistic patterns of thought. Later on, we shall also have to examine the difficulties it may present to a mind desirous of grasping the true significance of the immanence of Christ in the Universe and anxious at the same time not to derogate from the divine transcendence. Nevertheless, we do not believe that Teilhard's Christology is unorthodox; on the contrary, it seems to us fundamentally in agreement with the living faith of the Church, and there are few others which harmonize so well with the whole of the Holy Scripture.

To understand the Christology of Teilhard de Chardin it is essential to know the man himself, with his intensely integrated personality and his acute sense of the present.

Modern man suffers from a strange difficulty in feeling the present. Either he is incapable of maturing and perpetually in quest of change, or he is prematurely aged and a victim of the past and of conventional habits. In either case he flees from the present, and his image of Christ is mainly determined by the memories inherited from past generations. If Teilhard, as a palaeontologist and prehistorian, studied the past and took a passionate interest in it, it was fundamentally so far as the past threw light on the present and gave him a better grasp of its meaning. His personality, centred on the present, experienced with intensity its dimension of eternity. He sees Christ and lives him as a person really present in himself and in the World of which he is a part. In this Teilhard resembles the artists of the Middle Ages and the Renaissance who depicted Christ as their contemporary, because to them that is what he really was. The Christ whom the Church of his mother made known to him is not in old memories or in a theoretical doctrine, but in his personal experience of the real World which he encounters. And he knew this World as few men have known it, because he loved it as few men have loved it.

3. The expression "Christ the foundation of Cosmogenesis" is not Teilhard's, but it is a very fair summary of the Christology which emerges from his works, and, among others, from LE MILIEU DIVIN. In the second part of this book, he develops his thesis in the form of a syllogism:

*At the heart of our universe, each soul exists for God in our Lord.*

Teilhard is careful to stress that our belonging to the Lord must be understood in its full plenitude and mystic profundity: "(. . .) with the strengthening and purification of the reality and urgency contained in the most powerful interconnections revealed to us in every order of the physical and human world." (OEUVRES, Vol. 4, p. 44.)

*In our universe* (. . .) *all that is sensible, in its turn exists for the soul.* Teilhard insistently develops this minor premiss of his reasoning: "It is essential to see—to see things as they are and to see them really and intensely (. . .) to be aware of the extensions of our being throughout the world (. . .) to be astonished at the extent and intimacy of our relations with the Universe." (OEUVRES, Vol. 4, p. 44.) Man labours in the world, he knows himself and expresses himself through it, transforms it and spiritualizes it; without the presence of man, the world would lose its raison d'être.

As a consequence, "We must recognize," writes Teilhard, "that in the whole process which from first to last activates and directs the elements of the universe, everything forms a single whole. And we begin to see more distinctly the great sun of Christ the King, of Christ *amictus mundo*, of the universal Christ, rising over our interior world. Little by little, stage by stage, everything is finally linked to the supreme centre *in quo omnia constant.*" (OEUVRES, Vol. 4, p. 49.)

To sum up, we would say: Christ present at the origin of the creation of the world and at its end as its ultimate goal is also the permanent centre of attraction and unification. To the believer he is the foundation of Cosmogenesis.

4. Teilhard's Christology as we have just formulated it following the text of LE MILIEU DIVIN embodies no truly new proposition for a Christian. What is new is the link that connects the propositions. Teilhard's great merit has been to show that these truths, habitually accepted singly and independently, must be understood as a whole, not only by establishing interconnections between them, but by regarding them as different aspects of a single truth of a higher order. Moreover, this central verity cannot be regarded as a theoretical doctrine, however exalting and beautiful it may be, but must be made into a principle of action which will transform the life of Man and the history of the World.

After LE MILIEU DIVIN, which, it should not be forgotten, was written in 1926, we find that his Christology develops, becomes more profound, is integrated more explicitly in his vision of the world, and ends by acquiring its final and original form. In the years which followed, Teilhard was led to the discovery that the World, the Universe as the extension of Man, possesses a new dimension, which had so far escaped detection, and the minor premiss of the syllogism proposed in LE MILIEU DIVIN was to be profoundly modified as a result. The World is in evolution, and evolution is the fundamental law of nature; it extends even to Man, and, far from ceasing there, attains in Man its most sublime rebound, making him converge on point Omega and emerge into Eternity.

We have explained at length elsewhere what evolution means to Teilhard de Chardin as a fundamental law of the Universe, how it transposes itself at the level of Man, and how, in a Mankind capable of realizing the movement of planetization, this same law of evolution opens up the prospect of an emergence into the transcendent.[1] This is not the moment to repeat it. But it is worth emphasizing that, in our opinion, Teilhard's most original and most personal contribution was to make us conscious of the fundamental importance of the law of evolution in understanding Man's place in nature and the meaning of being.

5. It seems to us that he himself only acquired total certainty on this subject after the discovery of the Sinanthropus at Chou kou tien. For by confirming beyond discussion the significance of the Pithecanthropus unearthed at Java, this discovery swept away all hesitations about the continuity of the animal origin and of the origin of Man. But by a reversal of perspective which was normal to Teilhard's mentality, evolution, which had hitherto appeared to be a law of natural science, acquired from its application to Man a general philosophical significance, and became a principle of intelligibility for the whole Universe right up to the atomic elements. Thus evolution, from being a simple biological law became, by embracing Man, a Cosmological law. This profoundly changed the meaning of the World—of the Universe as an extension of Man—referred to in the minor premiss of the syllogism in LE MILIEU DIVIN. It is now very different from that Universe of well ordered and regular movements known to Copernicus and Galileo, very different from the Universe governed by the laws of the conservation of matter and of energy. The Universe of evolution is

[1] *The World Vision of Teilhard de Chardin*, TEILHARD REVIEW, Nos. 1 and 2, 1966, or INTERNATIONAL PHILOSOPHICAL QUARTERLY, Vol. 1, No. 4, December 1961.

one where the multiple takes precedence over the simple, where movement is given value only by its functions, where accumulation engenders order and where complexity, by unification, gives birth to the
new, and, finally and above all, it has become a Universe dominated by
what Teilhard calls the "Phenomenon of Man". It is a World where Man
is paramount, not only in the thinking of spiritual philosophy, but also
in the eyes of the naturalist and the scientist. It may be noted that the
volume which he published under the title THE PHENOMENON OF MAN
dates from 1948 and the article with the same title from 1930, the year
in which he also published one of the first articles on *Sinanthropus
Pekinensis*. One can realize the impact which this discovery must have
had on him by comparing the spirit and vocabulary of the writings
dating back before 1929, like LE MILIEU DIVIN or *Palaeontology and the
Appearance of Man* (OEUVRES, Vol. 2, p. 51) with later ones like THE
PHENOMENON OF MAN.

6. If the minor premiss of the syllogism is modified because Man,
and the World to which he belongs, are henceforth united by the same
dynamics of evolution, the major premiss also finds itself transformed
in similar fashion. In effect, if Man and the Universe, which belong to
Christ, are borne along by an upward movement of evolution, this can
only be because Christ himself is its immanent and transcendent centre.
What has proved to be the fundamental law of the Universe, of which
Man is the culminating expression, must necessarily be found eminently
in Christ. Thus we find the verification of how Christ, in whom all
things consist, can speak of himself as the Alpha and Omega of creation,
of how, in other words, Christ can be the centre of Cosmogenesis.

The concept of evolution, originating in the life sciences, after
penetrating the philosophic domain of Man's relations with the world,
has now entered the theological domain of Man's relations with God.
Teilhard was not the pioneer. A century earlier, as Ernst Benz pointed
out, John Henry Newman undertook to demonstrate the existence of
evolution in theology by his study ON THE DEVELOPMENT OF DOCTRINE.
It is true that this essay dealt only with the evolution of dogma, and
even that very cautiously. Moreover, when it came to formulating the
argument of substance, Newman contented himself with a long quotation from a contemporary author, Butler. But the idea of evolution is
there, very definitely present in Newman's mind. In fact, and this
might incite the scientists to a certain modesty when they speak of
theologians, Newman used the concept of evolution in theology some

years before it was launched in the natural sciences: Newman's treatise on the development of dogma appeared in 1845 and THE ORIGIN OF SPECIES not until 1859, and Wallace's essay in 1858.

7. One might gain the impression from the foregoing that Teilhard's Christology developed, in the last analysis, under the influence of scientific discoveries. The theory of the evolution of species being verified at the level of Man, he might seem to have made it a general principle for the interpretation of the Universe not only on the cosmological and philosophical plane, but also on the plane of theology, and, in particular, of Christology. This interpretation, which seems to be suggested by the reasoning followed here, only indicates one single element in Teilhard's thought, and what seems to be an external and secondary element, which reflects the path he took to make his vision of Christ understood by others, rather than the expression of his own manner of conceiving it. A reading of Teilhard's writings, especially those before 1929, like LE MILIEU DIVIN leads us to believe that in his innermost thoughts he reasoned conversely; he believed in the World in relation to Man, as he believed in Man in relation to his faith in Christ, and he believed in Universal evolution because he had discovered it in Christ.

For the rest, this is also implied by the type of reasoning we have just been considering. It would be a mistake to think that we can leave it where we broke off, since it is still incomplete.

8. After mounting upward from below, we must now reverse our perspective and consider from above, starting from Christ himself, what is the meaning of man and the whole Universe evolving towards Christ. Just as Christ exists all for God, so Man exists all for Christ, and the entire Universe evolves and converges in order to realize the plenitude of the stature of Christ in Man. It is in evolution because Christ is in growth.

Opening Volume IX of the COLLECTED WORKS in search of a quotation from Teilhard to illustrate the argument, we fell upon a page of the essay entitled 'Mon Univers' which dates from 1924:

"The Christian has only to meditate on his Credo to find in the Revelation which he accepts, the unhoped-for realization of the dream to the threshold of which philosophy logically leads him. I want to show in this chapter that Christianity assumes its full value in the light of the ideas of creative Union (i.e. Evolution in Teilhard's sense) to such an extent that this theory, instead of being regarded as a philosophy confirmed and strengthened by Christian views, deserves rather to be described as a philosophical extension of faith in the Incarnation.

"For the sake of brevity let us give the name Omega to the supreme cosmic Term revealed by creative Union.

"Everything I have to say comes down to three points:

"1. Christ revealed is nothing but Omega.

"2. It is as Omega that he presents himself as palpable and as inevitable in all things.

"3. And finally, it is in order to be constituted Omega that he had, by the labours of his Incarnation, to conquer and animate the Universe." (OEUVRES, Vol. IX, p. 81.)

After this clear and explicit text there is no need to look further. Teilhard shows that, if from below upwards evolution is centred on Omega, looked at from above, starting from Christ, Cosmogenesis becomes a Christogenesis, or, as he says a little further on, alluding to the words of the sacrament of the Eucharist: "Nothing labours in creation except for the purpose of aiding, near or far, in the consecration of the Universe." (OEUVRES, Vol. IX, p. 94.)

9. What place is occupied in this vision of Christ, the Pleroma of the Universe, by the fact of the Incarnation and the historic Christ?

Let us start by clearing up any ambiguity which may underlie the word "historic". For a fact to be historic, it is not enough that it happened at a specific place and time so that the chronicler could record it. The important thing is that the event should influence history, that it should radiate in space and time and take shape as a landmark at the crossroads of mankind. In a historic fact universal influence is more important than location, and permanence in time than the exact date. From this point of view, Christ as a historic person has his place in Teilhard's vision of the World, and it is indeed central and unique. In the first place, the analysis of the Phenomenon of Man shows that Omega, to which Mankind must converge by the conscious acceptance of the universal attraction of spirits, must, if it is to be a centre of attraction for human beings, make itself known and manifest as Man, in other words there must be the Incarnation of the Divine. Secondly, Christ appearing on Earth came at a historical epoch when man was sufficiently spiritualized, had sufficiently recognized his person and his place in society to be able to conceive and prepare the rebound of evolution by the convergence of mankind at planetary level. We can therefore conclude that the historic Christ is the nucleus of the Christian Phenomenon in which the Phenomenon of Man reaches culmination.

10. After the question of the Incarnation comes the question of the place of Redemption in Teilhard's vision of Christ. There are two things which must be said here. Teilhard is consciously and deliberately optimistic. He is not unaware of sorrow, pain and evil in the world. But he looks upon them only as shortcomings in the ascent of evolution, and not as positive values in themselves. He knows that Christ died and that his death saved the world, and that in consequence the final success of evolution is a thing divinely guaranteed which no human malevolence can ever wreck. He does not whittle down hope to a consolation in bad moments. For him hope is the arrow of time that indicates the direction of evolution, the magnetic field which polarizes action. Teilhard knew perfectly well what death meant, but he believed above all in Resurrection and always hoped that he would die on Easter Day. This was granted to him on an April afternoon in 1955.

The second remark relates to the meaning of the word "Redemption". Theology in recent years has been actively concerned to clarify it. Christ's passion and death are no longer regarded as the price of blood to appease the divine wrath, but rather as a mystery of purification and unification, and the supreme expression of the gift of self, which, assumed by Christ, is capable of destroying the force of evil in the world and of developing the vital forces of progress.

In the light of these observations, Redemption holds a place in the vision of Christ proposed by Teilhard which is quite as singular as that of the Incarnation, since in the first place it is the pledge given from on high of the final success of evolution, and secondly it grants access to this success to all those who follow Christ and live more in Him.

In his essay 'Le Christ Evoluteur', written for his theologian colleagues, Teilhard purposely underlines the positive aspects of Redemption: "The Lamb of God bearing, with the sins, the weight of the progress of the World. The idea of pardon and of sacrifice transforming itself by self-enrichment into the idea of consummation and conquest. Christ the Redeemer fulfilling Himself, without detracting from his suffering countenance, in the dynamic plenitude of a Christ-Evolutive" (Cahier No. 5, p. 26). Just as it is the task of man, the culmination of the evolution of the world, to pursue its development, so it is the work of Christ, the crown of Mankind, to ensure its fulfilment by Elevation and Redemption. Or, in other words, while Man must pursue the evolution of the World, the fulfilment of the evolution of Mankind is the work of Christ the Redeemer.

11. The attraction of this vision of Christ lies not only in its rigorous unity, verifying that "in Christ all things consist" as St. Paul says, but also in the fact that this vision is fundamentally positive, oriented forward in the direction of progress and loaded with hope.

It has been said that Christianity offers a retrograde vision of the world, opposed to progress, and there have been Christians who have thought this and have even acted accordingly. Nevertheless, this attitude is fundamentally opposed to the spirit of the Church. We do not pretend that the Catholic Church, as a body, has always been the first to promote progress. On more than one occasion progress has been defended and propagated by its adversaries, but every time it has been in the name of Evangelical principles advocated and disseminated by the Church on the value and the indefeasible rights of man. Not only is there no conflict between Christianity and progress, but it must be said that Christianity is the only sure foundation for an ideology of progress. Many philosophers of history have shown this clearly enough, like Gustav Schnürer, Etienne Gilson and Christopher Dawson. Christianity, by exorcizing the spirits of nature, by placing man at the head of creation, created the essential preliminary conditions for scientific and technical progress; by asserting the equality of all men before God and the inalienable character of the rights of man, it is the basis of all social progress. But leaving aside the influence of Christianity on our conception of the world and the dignity of man, we must refer at this point to its influence on our conception of time and history. Unlike other religions which have a cyclical time composed of eras which follow and repeat each other, or which envisage a dissolution into nothingness, Christian time is one-way, irreversible and pointing to progress. This last point was decisive in the conversion of Newman. He wrote his treatise on the development of dogma precisely to explain to his Anglican friends how he had arrived at the conviction that the Church of Rome had shown itself faithful to progress while the others had remained conservative.

It is true that this progress was often regarded by Christians as invisible, in opposition to the World and with its goal and its term in the Beyond. But the Church has never allowed this point of view to be carried to the extreme and has always fought against Manichaean

tendencies. Furthermore, while during the last century we have witnessed an extraordinary upsurge of scientific, technical and social
progress, Christianity has become more and more conscious of its
obligations in this respect. Many Christian thinkers have concerned
themselves with these things and have tried to encourage their fellows
along the road of progress in all its forms.

12. But the pace of progress has outstripped the powers of assimilation of Christians who remain torn by the conflict between the visible
and the invisible, between the below and the beyond. The great merit
of Teilhard de Chardin is not only to have discovered and popularized
the concept of evolution as the explanation of man's place in the
Universe, or to have indicated how its application should be extended
to the sphere of religion, but to have shown that this concept enables
the Christian to discover an aspect of Christ which had previously been
overshadowed: Christ as the Centre of the Universe, animating the
ascent of the World by His Spirit. Teilhard has shown the Christian how
to feel quite at home in the world by finding Christ everywhere. He has
clearly and consistently shown that participating in Cosmogenesis and
working for progress advances Christogenesis and contributes to the
growth of Christ, and, furthermore, that there can be no true progress
which is not directed towards Christ and inspired by His Spirit.

Let us recognize that Teilhard's merit was great; the elaboration
of this vision of the World and of Christ demanded an intense and
prolonged effort of prayer and reflection, and while he wished to respond
to the light which he had seen, there proved to be very few who were
capable of understanding him. For a long time he was under suspicion,
he could never obtain permission to publish his works touching on
theology. But he believed too greatly in Christ Alpha and Omega of the
Universe-in-evolution not to be able to recognize his own "divine
milieu" and to remain faithful to it.

13. The outline we have just sketched of the Christology of
Teilhard de Chardin throws into highest relief the immanence of Christ
in the Universe of which he is the Centre of evolution, but it might
seem to some people to detract from his transcendence. In other words,
the Revelation of God, the Elevation of man by grace, Redemption, all
the gifts which theology describes as "supernatural" seem, from what
we have just seen, to arise out of evolution and result from the conditions and development of nature. To believe in Christ-Evolutive, as
Teilhard calls him, would be to do away with the distinction between

the natural and the supernatural order, to do away with the freedom of grace and thereby ignore the transcendence of God. The objection made arises out of a misunderstanding. It is true that Incarnation, Elevation, Redemption, are fundamentally free, the pure gifts of the divine goodness. For the transcendent God can only act freely. Now, the traditional school points out that the supernatural order of grace is free because it is an order wholly different and distinct from natural order, an order which is not in any way owed to human nature, either by constitution, or as a consequence, or on demand, or because of merits; in other words, man has no right to grace, either by his nature, or as a consequence of his nature, or because he is entitled to demand it, or because he may merit it. The final meaning of these negations is rationally to safeguard the gratuity of grace, that is to say, the total freedom of God in his act towards man.

This definition of the supernatural order makes us uncomfortable because, being entirely negative, it does not enlighten us about its content. We can also perceive that it is an idea inspired by Aristotle, in which the relation to natural order resembles the relation between form and matter. But need we really be worried about it? When all is said and done, the insistence on the distinction between natural order and supernatural order is designed to ensure the gratuity of God's act to man, since gratuity is the only attitude consistent with the transcendence of God.

14. What does the concept of gratuity mean? We have spoken of the traditional teaching that the gratuitous is that which is not due to the nature of a person or to his properties, which cannot be claimed, or even merited, what in a word, is in no way owing. This wholly negative definition, we have said, tells us little about what gratuity really is, and it is even too wide, since it could also be applied to the arbitrary, or to the gratuitous in the pejorative sense as when one speaks of a "gratuitous insult". What, then, is gratuity? Let us recognize that it is a first datum, and therefore difficult to define, but which we can still understand clearly and unambiguously in terms which might be expressed as follows: "Gratuity is the property which marks a personal gift so far as it is personal." A personal gift is that which originates with one person and is offered to another. So far as it is personal, it is total in its origin, total in its term and total also in its content, which cannot be anything other than the person himself, who, in giving it, gives himself. Such a gift is not determined by anything except the

loving spontaneity of the giver—of the one who gives himself. He is under no external necessity. If he appears influenced by the lovable character of the loved one to whom he offers the gift, it is in appearance only. The lovable character of the loved one is fundamentally determined by the one who loves, whose loving kindness creates it and keeps it alive. Such a personal gift proceeds entirely from the giver; it is absolute, totally spontaneous, or, in other words, gratuitous.

There is nothing, then, to prevent this gift from being written down somewhere; generosity does not vanish when the intention has been enshrined in a Will. The free gift of Salvation promised by God is not diminished because he confided his promise to the Patriarchs and the Prophets. Neither is it diminished because we are now capable, not without help from the Revelation he has accorded us, of perceiving, in looking back, that God has manifested himself in a certain way since the beginning of time in creation, and that he reveals himself up to the last elements in the movement of evolution which bears the whole Universe with it in an ascent which nothing can arrest, which proves to be constantly more and more powerful, and which culminates in the appearance of man, and which is now preparing under our very eyes for a new rebound centred on Omega, the plenitude of the revelation of Christ.

15. But here, it is true, a distinction must be made—and Teilhard was always careful to make it—Omega becomes Christ only by an act of faith, that is to say, an act of personal recognition which is only achieved in the encounter of the call of Christ and the submission of the man who hears it. Omega perceived as a personal principle in the prolongation of reflection on human planetization becomes a person in the authentic sense only by the mystic encounter which occurs when the man who has perceived the presence of the other submits to deliver himself up totally, that is to say, to believe in him. This act is similar to that of two people who deliver themselves up spiritually to each other in total reciprocity, and each, creating by their mutual faith the lovable character of the other, constitute by that very fact what we call amity. In this way the distinction between the natural and supernatural order is maintained and even accentuated, but conceived in a personalistic manner.

We have said that Omega becomes Christ only by an act of faith, but we have also shown that a purely external interpretation of the Universe could not disclose either the meaning of evolution or the presence of Omega at the focus of creative unification. To achieve this we must open ourselves to the influence of a personal presence. Thus, all those who have opened their eyes to the evolution of the World and of Mankind have already consented to submit to the hidden presence of Christ in the Universe, and by accepting the existence of Cosmogenesis are preparing themselves to recognize the reality of Christogenesis.

16. We can conclude that the Christology of Teilhard de Chardin cannot be separated from his vision of the World; that in mounting in spirit from the evolution of Matter towards Man and projecting forward and inwards the rebound of evolution which manifests itself in the planetization of mankind, we can see, rising on the horizon, Omega, the focus of Universal evolution, which reveals itself to the man who is prepared to encounter it as the person of Christ the Redeemer. But above all we have been able to recognize that it is only in appearance that the spirit mounts from Matter to Christ, and that in reality Teilhard de Chardin's vision of the World is a Cosmogenesis inspired by Christogenesis, or, in other words, a Christology.

# CHAPTER SEVEN

## A Radio Discussion*

Vernon Sproxton in the Chair

VERNON SPROXTON Gentlemen, Father Teilhard is the only religious thinker of modern times who has had a society, indeed societies, founded to examine and expound his work. What are the reasons for the current vogue in Teilhard? Dr. Cuénot.

DR. CUÉNOT I think there are good reasons for it. Teilhard had an intuition of the special needs of his time. He knew what anguish is, and he felt the anguish of other people, and he tried to reconcile mankind with itself. He tried to explain to them the main ideas of Christian religion, but in the language of the twentieth century.

VERNON SPROXTON Father Elliott, why do you think his thought appeals particularly to scientists?

FR. ELLIOTT I think it is because he has shown that it is possible to understand the world, taking scientific experience, and specially scientific experience on evolution, as a starting point and as a key to understanding man's place in the universe. I think his way of looking at the world is a way which has a certain kinship with scientific thinking.

VERNON SPROXTON Dr. Fothergill, would you support that?

DR. FOTHERGILL I think that Teilhard appeals particularly to ordinary people, the man in the street. Teilhard himself wrote about a certain anguish among human beings at the present time. And when ordinary people read his books they find that this anguish gradually diminishes.

VERNON SPROXTON   So, in fact, you would say his thought exercizes almost a pastoral function to the intellect?

DR. FOTHERGILL   Yes. Teilhard wasn't a priest in the pastoral sense. He was a scientist, he was a palaeontologist, and perhaps he was doing this more or less unconsciously without knowing it.

VERNON SPROXTON   I have a suspicion that he hasn't really caught on in the intellectual areas of our country's life. Do you think, Bernard Towers, that the intellectual establishment at the moment has got an inbuilt prejudice against his ideas, and, if so, why?

BERNARD TOWERS   I think the intellectual establishment as we know it in this country at the moment has got an inbuilt prejudice against anyone who crosses too many barriers, as it were, in one leap. Science and philosophy in this country have developed, over the last hundred years, into a series of very highly specialized studies. This, of course, is very necessary for the development of science, for the development of ideas. But one drawback is that a man engaged professionally in such work would feel it might be a handicap to him if he were thought to be engaging in ideas beyond his narrow field of competence. Therefore I think a large number of our scientists would feel hesitant about getting involved in discussion of such great ideas as those of Teilhard. But I think at the same time one ought to make the point that there are in this country some of the most eminent scientists, particularly in the biological field, who are very concerned with the study of Teilhard's works. And I think the time is going to come, in the latter part of this century, when we shall see their interest and their influence growing more and more.

VERNON SPROXTON   Is there, Anthony Dyson, a similar inbuilt prejudice against Teilhard amongst the theologians and philosophers, for instance?

ANTHONY DYSON   Perhaps one could draw a distinction here between theologians and philosophers. I think the philosophers perhaps are somewhat suspicious of Teilhard because of the strong empiricist and positivist tradition in English philosophy, which has been active for some time. As far as the theologians are concerned perhaps the reasons are slightly different. Philosophical theology, or philosophy of religion, or dogmatic theology have not in fact played a very big role in English theology, at least since the nineteenth century. The *forte* of the English theologians has been very much biblical criticism. But these are very early days, as far as Teilhard is concerned. His writings have not all appeared, there are problems of translation, the style is somewhat difficult, and some English people, I think, find this very unsympathetic. I think the immediate future promises a situation in which Teilhard's thought will be found to be much more congenial. We have only to think of the new subjects which are being introduced into the theological faculties—such as sociology of religion, relations between religion and science, and so on—to realize that it's in this sort of work that Teilhard's thought will become extremely important in the next few years.

VERNON SPROXTON   M. Garaudy, what is it in Teilhard's thinking which has made it an attractive field for dialogue with the Marxists?

PROF. GARAUDY   I think, as my friend Cuénot said, that the main reason for Teilhard's success is that he has succeeded in explaining what is fundamental in the Christian message, in the language of our time, in terms of the world vision of our time. For us Marxists we have someone to talk with who believes in social transformation and continually appeals for an unceasing metamorphosis of man. Man continually going beyond himself towards his own future. We find in Teilhard the optimism of a true master of *joie de vivre*. He does not present the world to us as a vale of tears where men's main pre-occupation would consist in expiating a primordial sin, but rather sees the world as a construction site for the future in which we are to construct confidently human unity. These themes, naturally, a Marxist finds congenial.

H

VERNON SPROXTON    Dr. Cuénot, have you any light to cast on this question about why, on a first reading of the situation at any rate, some of his views seem to get an unsympathetic reaction in Britain at the moment?

DR. CUÉNOT    Teilhard was something of an Anglo-Saxon. He is not quite French. I think he has felt the influence of Anglo-Saxon pragmatism, and one thing is certain: Teilhard has nothing at all of the Cartesian, thanks to God. I wonder why there are difficulties in England about him, since THE PHENOMENON OF MAN is the continuation of a very long theological and scientific effort to reconcile Darwinism and the Christian faith, which began very soon after the publication of THE ORIGIN OF SPECIES, of animal species. You find, well, I should say perhaps a dozen sketches of THE PHENOMENON OF MAN either in England, or in New England in the States, and even in Germany, and so it's possible to say that Teilhard belongs to English thought. Of course he knew nothing of it, and he thought by himself, but still the kinship is very striking.

VERNON SPROXTON    I think it was Helmut De Terra who said, in the book he wrote about life in the field with him, that Teilhard's scientific work gave the impression that Teilhard had already formulated his views, and was waiting for external observation to show them to be well founded. Is there any truth in this contention?

FR. ELLIOTT    I think there is a certain truth in it. My first impression, I would say, had been that the world vision of Teilhard de Chardin had arisen from science, from the notion of evolution as discovered in biological science; and that this notion of evolution became for him a key notion to interpret the meaning of man in the universe. But reading his writings of the early years, it is quite clear that he had this notion because of his belief in the meaning of Christ as the centre of the universe, and that he later found in the scientific discoveries confirmation of what was a primordial view of Christ as the centre of the world, the one in whom everything consists, as has said St. Paul; so I think that the idea proposed is in fact basically true.

VERNON SPROXTON  This looks as though he invested some of his scientific empirical discoveries with a teleology which wasn't inherent?

DR. TOWERS  Well, I think here it's a question as to what level of hypothesis you're dealing with. Science always works through the hypothetico-deductive method. One must have a hypothesis to work on, deduce certain consequences of that hypothesis, and then appeal to the phenomena to invalidate the hypothesis or to support it. To this extent, I think Teilhard was working simply as any other scientist works. He had a hypothesis of very great generality. Well then, he observed very objectively the phenomena in order to see whether these phenomena supported the hypothesis or would lead him to reject it.

VERNON SPROXTON  But would you say that there was any qualitative distinction between the sort of religious faith judgement, about the ultimate end of the universe, which Teilhard used to inform some of his scientific work, and the kind of much more proximate faith judgements about the general working of natural laws and so on that the scientist uses?

DR. TOWERS  Well, of course, Teilhard can't escape from his own personality. He had this great religious feeling, a great religious hypothesis. This in turn was bound to affect the way in which he looked at natural phenomena. This one must accept; but I don't think that this in any way discredits him as a scientist.

VERNON SPROXTON  Would you like to say something about this, Dr. Cuénot?

DR. CUÉNOT  In the first world war he may be considered above all as a theologian, and a mystic. And afterwards he started positive science, and very patiently he tried to check his mystical and theological and philosophical ideas, and tried to build a dialectic to explain the phenomenon of socialization, so he has checked all his religious ideas. It could have brought him to spiritual catastrophe. It didn't. To my mind it was a success, and that's the reason why his science had such an importance for him. He had no water-tight compartments; and his science offered him a vision of the world which confirmed him partly in his mystical ideas and philosophical ideas.


VERNON SPROXTON   Dr. Fothergill, as you read the more scientific bits of Teilhard's work, do you think he loads phenomena with teleological reason which is not really borne out by the empirical facts?


DR. FOTHERGILL   Perhaps this is a fault of Teilhard's writing, and one of the reasons perhaps why some of the scientists and the philosophers and the theologians criticize him. He seems to them to be committing the cardinal sin of bringing together science and philosophy in the same context—in the same sentence almost. And to a certain extent this is true. But it's a special style of Teilhard. And if one wants to understand Teilhard, one's got to forgive him this, and read behind what he says in order to get his meaning.


DR. TOWERS   May I just comment on this question of teleology? Teleology, of course, is a dirty word these days in science. Although many scientists actually use teleological arguments, they nearly always find it necessary to introduce the argument with a phrase such as "at the risk of appearing teleological". I am an anatomist—which is one of the most objective of all sciences. Some years ago I wrote a paper on teleology and the anatomist, and in it I tried to distinguish different meanings which different writers have given to the word "teleology". The word of course itself—telos—simply means an "end". Now the word "end" clearly conveys two quite distinct meanings. If you say that you take a "final examination", for instance, that phrase means two things: one is that you are taking an examination at the end of a period of time, you are completing a course of study. But the other meaning, implicit in the phrase, is that it was with this object in view that you undertook the course of study. So the word telos, or the word final, always has these two meanings: one of which is an end result, and the other is an end in view. Science is concerned with end results, and this is what one might call a radical teleology, a radical finality. Now, I think that Teilhard is most of the time looking at science in this way. He is observing what has happened, and is saying: this is the end result that has been achieved. He then extrapolates into the future and says: if this trend is to continue, what is likely to be the ultimate result? Well, then he introduces a sort of end in view idea.

VERNON SPROXTON   When he talks about consciousness in inanimate things, now, what evidence is there for this?

DR. TOWERS   Well, if you are a thorough-going evolutionist, then the problem is how far back in the history of the world are you to take the concept of consciousness? If it is evident there in higher mammalian forms, it's also evident in all other vertebrate forms, in invertebrate forms. If amoeba reacts to a stimulus, then it is reacting in a sense which it would be legitimate to describe as giving evidence of consciousness. Is it not present there, as Teilhard says it is, in the propensity that atoms show for electrons to unite with protons? This gives a sort of interiority to the atom, which is not present in the individual electron. Teilhard would merely extend the notion of consciousness right back to that level.

DR. FOTHERGILL   Could I have a come back here? Scientists, philosophers and theologians—everybody starts with ideas. And, of course, Teilhard did the same. So the answer to Helmut De Terra's question was that Teilhard did this. But, we must remember also at the same time, Teilhard was a man with a strong sense of his religion, and he realized that all things would ultimately end in Christ; that was part of his faith. And I think it was this realization which led him to develop the dialectic of evolution. And he develops this dialectic consistently throughout practically all of his books, that is he starts with emergence, we then have divergence, and ultimately, at the human phase, we have convergence, in which it is possible for all things to end in Christ.

VERNON SPROXTON    Right, let's turn to his Christology, because if, in fact, the universe is necessarily evolving, moving forward to a place where Christ is all in all, what really is the point and place of the mission of Jesus Christ? Could you say something, Father Elliott?

FR. ELLIOTT    Well, I would make a comment on the word "necessarily". I do not think we could state it in this way. Of course, the whole of evolution is going towards a higher convergence, and Teilhard finds in the general trend of evolution the thrust which he thinks is so strong that a failure is impossible. At the human level, failure becomes possible; and this is what we call sin; and sin exists in the world and endangers the success of evolution. We believe that once man has sinned, he's not able by his own force to restore the situation. There we see the place of Christ, Redeemer, coming in the world to make sure that man can restore this situation which he has destroyed himself. The place of Christ, in this view of the world in evolution, the place of Christ is that he first is Omega, the centre, the focus of evolution, who became visible. I mean Christ incarnated. That's the way I would interpret this meaning of "necessarily".

DR. TOWERS    Yes. Because in man he recognizes a free individual who is capable now of directing the course of evolution; and could completely make evolution meaningless in the sense that he could destroy all life; but now for Teilhard, he says if man is to complete himself, then he has an option before him, but man himself must make this choice, and there is nothing necessary about the choice that he may make.

VERNON SPROXTON    Well, there is a sense, isn't there, in which the New Testament says look, it's all over, it's completed, because in Jesus

Christ you have there the new creation, who is a discontinuous intrusion on the plane of history, and there's good New Testament ground at any rate for saying that the battle really about man's ultimate fulfilment, beatification or whatever you like to say, was fought out and won there. Now how does this square up with Teilhard's evolutionary view?

FR. ELLIOTT   This battle was fought out and won in Christ himself but not in the world; and it is yet the function, the duty of every man to choose to enter in Christ, to follow him, so that this triumph which is only inchoate, only a beginning in Christ, could really become the triumph of mankind; but it will depend on the acceptance of every man and of mankind as a whole.

VERNON SPROXTON   Several people have said that Teilhard's view of the future, particularly in view of the terrible things which were about to descend upon Europe, was so naive—his optimism—that it almost wasn't true. Now, would you say that Teilhard was a naive optimist?

PROF. GARAUDY   I do not think that one can accuse Teilhard of naive optimism. He often foresees the possibility of the failure of evolution, and he bids us realize the fact that we are responsible for the failure or the success of this evolution. There resides here the possibility not of a naive but of a militant optimism. Militant—that is to say, an optimism which exalts the beauty and dignity of the world—not of the world as it is, but of the world which can emerge and can be constructed by our efforts, our intelligence, and our courage.

DR. CUÉNOT   Teilhard has the optimism of a man, of a Christian, who believes in the resurrection of Christ. And that is very important. But one must underline that Teilhard's optimism is a dramatic one. Of course, he is no pessimist, but still he has lived through a drama, and one feels this drama in his optimism.

VERNON SPROXTON    When we put together some of Father Teilhard's thought and some of the New Testament, I think the man can be excused who thinks that there is a dichotomy between the two. An optimist will say: it's going to be all right on the night. This is a bad dress rehearsal, but it's going to be all right on the night. Now, the Bible as it seems to me, when it contemplates what is going to happen in history at the end, says: now look, it's *not* going to be all right on the night, it's going to be incomparably worse than any of you can imagine. It is going to be catastrophic. Some of Teilhard's views seem to contradict this central biblical doctrine. Anthony, would you like to say a word about this?


ANTHONY DYSON    I think it's extremely difficult in these respects to talk about *a* biblical view of eschatology. We have to realize, for example, that the apocalyptic view of a catastrophic end of the world arose in the first place from the disastrous history of the Jews in the Old Testament. And arose from reflection upon that. But there is another view of eschatology in the Old Testament, a view which we might call the Davidic view of eschatology, which does look forward to a future where, as it were, all manner of things shall be well. And where it will not be brought about by a catastrophe but by a fulfil-ment of this world. Similarly, while there is certainly one sense in which the New Testament understands the work of Christ as decisive, as having happened once for all in human history, there are many other strands in the New Testament which indicate that we are to bring Christ's work to fulfilment in the world; and we have this whole area of thought in the Epistles to the Ephesians and the Colossians of the cosmic vision of Christ which encompasses the beginning and the present and the end of things. And he is not, in one sense, com-plete and his task is not complete, until he is all in all. It is perfectly consonant with the New Testament to hold that Christ's appearance in the world is not to be viewed as an anomaly, as a strange incursion into the world; but rather that this belongs to the whole plan of God for His cosmos. So I would certainly feel that there is no sign at all in Teilhard's thought that he is trying to diminish the person and the work of Christ, but rather that he is trying to draw out from the New Testament all the affirmations about the person of Christ and understand these anew in an evolutionary perspective.

VERNON SPROXTON   Is there any justification in the criticism that his view of convergence doesn't give original sin, as classically conceived, the place that it ought to have in his scheme of thought? After all, it was this, wasn't it, that brought him up pretty strongly against his Order; and actually involved his being sent to China for a while.

DR. CUÉNOT   Teilhard de Chardin has been reflecting on original sin, but I think he has given it a new cosmic and collective meaning. The origin of creation is not a catastrophe. But he says, and he stresses the fact, that an evolutive creation is something very fragile, if I should say, and especially at the level of mankind, of man, because man possesses this liberty which makes his greatness, and which makes him able to refuse God and to commit deicide. So I don't think that Teilhard has tried to diminish original sin. He makes it more important because it is cosmic—cosmic and collective. So we are all responsible. We are not able to say that if we had been Adam, we should not have sinned. It is a legend to say that Teilhard disdained, even didn't see, evil. Teilhard has often lived in a kind of existential anguish, which may be compared to that of Kierkegaard and the existentialists. For a philosopher who has no deep notion of evil, there is no anguish; there is none, for instance, in the philosopher Spinoza. But for a man who feels anguish, that shows that he has a quite clear vision of evil in the world.

VERNON SPROXTON   Would we all agree that in terms of the way Lucien Goldman has re-interpreted the wide Marxist position in France, that we are all embarqued, and there is a risk in the end that Teilhardians, Protestants and non-Teilhardians, Christians, we are all in the end justified by an affirmation in faith, in the movement of the universe towards its Christ in all?

DR. CUÉNOT   Well, there is no doubt that there is in Teilhard an act of faith. Because his whole philosophy is a series of acts of faith. An act of faith in the value of the world; the value of spirit; in the existence of God and the existence of Christ. But it is quite impossible to prove scientifically that the world is good; that the world evolves towards a victory of spirit.

ANTHONY DYSON    It seems to me that Teilhard in the last resort says
that our confidence about the outcome of the world depends upon an
act of faith; that the world is ultimately intelligible and has meaning;
and he comes to that act of faith ultimately by his faith as a Christian,
certainly not an act of faith which allows us any quietism, or any ease
in Zion; but much rather this act of faith commits us to act in the
world, and to bring the world to the conclusion which God has
destined for it.


DR. TOWERS    And his faith in human progress is precisely the ground on
which it has become possible for us now to establish dialogue with
Marxist thinkers, because here we have yet another strand in human
thought which is looking to the future and which has confidence in
the future, and here on this common ground we can work together.

*Printed with acknowledgements to the B.B.C.*

* The foregoing discussion was unscripted and is here printed as recorded. Eds.

# THE ASSOCIATION

There is a growing awareness of the relevance and importance of Teilhard's thought all over the world. Many social topics of the greatest significance are discussed by him in the context of scientific analyses of the evolutionary process. The implications of his theories are very far-reaching for the future of man. They need to be studied and discussed in relation to every aspect of human society.

The Association is an educational organisation whose activities include:

Organising study groups throughout Great Britain and Ireland
Arranging meetings, conferences and symposia
Setting up a central library and archives
Providing an information service to all enquirers
Publishing twice yearly THE TEILHARD REVIEW—free to members
Promoting films, television and radio broadcasts
Promoting the publication of a study series THE TEILHARD STUDY LIBRARY
Maintaining contacts with Associations in other countries pursuing similar aims
Encouraging the growth of affiliated Associations in the Commonwealth

To further these activities the Association must rely on voluntary donations, especially through the subscription of members, where possible by Deed of Covenant. You are invited to assist the Association's work through membership and participation in its activities. Minimum subscriptions are:

Ordinary Members    Two guineas per annum
Group Members       Five guineas per annum
Student Members     One guinea per annum

THE PIERRE TEILHARD DE CHARDIN ASSOCIATION
OF GREAT BRITAIN AND IRELAND

3 Cromwell Place, London S.W.7          (Telephone 01.584 7734)

# A FURTHER READING LIST

By Pierre Teilhard de Chardin, S.J.

THE PHENOMENON OF MAN, Collins, 25s; Fontana 5s
LE MILIEU DIVIN, Collins, 18s; Fontana 3s 6d
THE FUTURE OF MAN, Collins, 30s
LETTERS FROM A TRAVELLER, Collins, 25s; Fontana 5
HYMN OF THE UNIVERSE, Collins, 18s
THE MAKING OF A MIND: Letters from a Sol·
    Collins, 28s
THE APPEARANCE OF MAN, Collins, 25s
MAN'S PLACE IN NATURE, Collins, 18s
THE VISION OF THE PAST, Collins, 30s
TEILHARD ALBUM, Collins, 63s
HUMAN ENERGY, Collins, 25s
BUILDING THE EARTH, Geoffrey Chapm

---

TEILHARD DE CHARDIN: A Biographical Study, by Cla·         ·not
    Burns & Oates, 1965, 42s
TEILHARD DE CHARDIN AND THE MYSTERY OF CHRIST, by Christopher F.
    Mooney, S.J., Collins, 1966, 30s
THE RELIGION OF TEILHARD DE CHARDIN, by Henri de Lubac, S.J.
    Collins, 1967, 42s
TEILHARD DE CHARDIN: SCIENTIST AND SEER, by C. E. Raven
    Collins, 1962, 25s
TEILHARD DE CHARDIN, by Bernard Towers
    Lutterworth Press, 1967, 6s
FROM ANATHEMA TO DIALOGUE, by Roger Garaudy, with an Introduction
    by Karl Rahner, S.J., and an Epilogue by J. B. Metz
    Collins, 1967, 25s

# INDEX OF NAMES

Numbers in italics refer to footnotes